mafia marriage

MY STORY

ROSALIE BONANNO
WITH BEVERLY DONOFRIO

St. Martin's Paperbacks

This is a true story. However, for the sake of preserving privacy, the names of certain nonpublic figures have been changed.

MAFIA MARRIAGE

Copyright © 1990 by Armeda Limited.
Wedding photograph on cover courtesy Ida Arts Studio. Published by arrangement with the author.
Cover photograph of frame on lace © Herman Estevez.

Library of Congress Catalog Card Number: 90-40321

ISBN: 0-312-97925-8

Printed in the United States of America

William Morrow Hardcover edition published 1990
Avon Books edition / October 1991
St. Martin's Paperbacks edition / March 2003

St. Martin's Paperbacks are published by St. Martin's Press, 175 Fifth Avenue, New York, NY 10010.

10 9 8 7 6 5 4 3 2 1

For our children—
Chuck, Joe, Tore, and Gigi—
who were there and know

PREFACE

The idea for this book was conceived almost twenty years ago when my husband, Bill, was an inmate in the Federal Correctional Institution on Terminal Island, in the middle of Los Angeles harbor. He had received a letter from a woman in England who had read Gay Talese's *Honor Thy Father,* the best-selling nonfiction book in which Bill was the central focus. She said she felt I deserved a bouquet, or some such accolade, for the way I had managed to deal with that stressful period in our lives. Since Gay had touched on only a small part of my involvement, Bill felt there remained a much bigger story to be told. I said forget it. There was no way I could ever reveal my innermost feelings to strangers through an autobiography.

Then, in 1974, a breakthrough, so to speak, occurred when Robert Dellinger, a television and motion-picture screenwriter, came to Campbell, California, on special assignment for the *Los Angeles Times* to write a story about Bill's reintegration into society and his college lecture tour. It was during those interviews that I was able to talk—for the very first time—to an outsider. Bob said he felt

I should try to put on paper a woman's point of view about a side of life that, up to then, had not been exposed.

Once again I said, "Forget it." But Bob didn't give up. Over the next ten years he kept working on me: suggesting I keep notes, examine my feelings, write about those things that interested me.

Bill, too, kept encouraging me to write, to tell how I had struggled with the contrasts in our colorful and often contentious personalities. After all, he said, an autobiography is not just a simple chronological listing of the facts; it is a portrait, in words, of the feelings and emotions of a person in conflict, or harmony, with themselves, and the world around them. Although I was telling him I was growing warmer to the idea, I was still ambivalent. I was also fearful of the reactions of relatives and our children.

Then, in 1983, my father-in-law, Joseph Bonanno, published his autobiography, *A Man of Honor*. I was deeply moved by Dad's words. It gave me new and fresh insight into the traditions of family and the culture in which I was reared. And it nudged me closer to making a decision to go forward. As the reader will soon learn, I have never been one to just jump into a thing without giving it careful thought.

Finally, in 1986, my husband and Bob convinced me the timing was right for a TV movie about my experiences as a wife and daughter in a life-style that was fading from the scene. In particular, Bill believed I would have the opportunity to differentiate—in the minds of millions of TV viewers—the subtle but distinct differences between the mafia and the Mafia. The historic mafia, with the lower case "m," meant to us, the Sicilian traditions involving old-fashioned family values like love, loyalty, fidelity, honor, and respect. However, it had been the tabloid treatment of the word, which almost always boldfaced every letter, that had changed Mafia into a symbol of violence and disregard for the law, a distortion of the original meaning we had known.

I agreed to go forward with the project. But I still was not comfortable with placing a magnifying glass on my life for everyone to see.

It was an alien world, that first exposure to Hollywood, "taking meetings" with production company and network executives. But the way was smoothed by Mickey Freiberg, my agent, whose total support surprised me since I believed those associated with Hollywood were clichéd and superficial. During negotiations with a major network (which later fell through), word leaked back to publishers in New York that there was a new "mafia" picture in the making. Slowly at first, then more rapidly, interest built and inquiries came. The publishers wanted to see the manuscript for the book. However, the truth of the matter was, there was no manuscript, just an outline for a script that had been formed by Bob and Bill over the years; a "pitch piece," as they say. It was a new role and experience for me: to be the focus of so much attention from executives who wanted to hear what I had to say. I found it intimidating, confusing, enlightening, and just a little exciting. Bill handled my new business relationships with an understanding I had not experienced before, though he did cock an eyebrow when I *told* him Mickey and I were flying to New York together to meet with Sterling Lord, a prominent literary agent. That trip, with two handsome men escorting me around the Big Apple, was a first for me and turned out to be successful. Our meetings with editors at William Morrow and Company resulted in a contract for this book. It was, by far, the easiest part of the project. Had I known at the time the pain and effort it would require to make this a reality, I would never have agreed to do it. Many, many times I wanted to give up, but Bill, Bob, Mickey, and Sterling encouraged me to stay with it.

There are many people to thank for helping make this a reality. My deepest appreciation goes to Beverly Donofrio, my co-author, for her patience, understanding, and writing skills. Her gentle questioning, support, and sympathetic manner opened up areas that had been long suppressed.

And even though it may read as if I am sometimes unduly hard on those I love the most, especially my husband, Bill, I could not have made it without his meaningful help. True to his nature and style, he was a pillar of strength and never failed to offer an idea or suggestion that helped improve the finished product.

I am indebted to my mother for those little remembrances that make those sections from my childhood a vivid and pleasant excursion into the past. And I would be remiss not to mention the Sisters at Mount St. Mary's, who also contributed.

A project of this scope demands many anecdotes, so I am especially grateful to my children— Chuck, Joe, Tore, and Gigi—as well as my daughters-in-law, Kathleen and Deborah, for responding to my pleas for colorful moments that had faded with the passing of time. They also were there when my enthusiasm sagged.

For their special interest and support, I wish to thank Jim Landis, Jill Hamilton, Lori Ames, and Pat Golbitz; Nick Mazzella for a beautiful photo section; and Linda Kosarin and those in the Art Department for creating a cover that got the word "mafia" right.

Credit for transcribing many hours of interview tapes goes to Patricia Cross, my neighbor and friend. And to Joel Turtle, Robert Castle, Joseph Gotter, and Mark Metzger, whose counsel I greatly appreciate.

Thank you, Bob Dellinger, Mickey Freiberg, Sterling Lord, and Jim Landis; you always had my best interests at heart.

And finally, once again, for Bill, who was there when I needed him. No matter what, you will always be my cowboy from out of the West.

—ROSALIE BONANNO

*mafia
marriage*

CHAPTER 1

WHEN I arrived in Mexico, I was met at the airport by a friend of my husband's who told me he would take me to Bill. The first thing I saw when I entered the restaurant was "Felice Cumpleaños, Rosalia" written on a banner. There were daisies, my favorite flower, in wine bottles placed in the middle of every table. Mexicans playing guitars began a love ballad, and when my husband walked out of the kitchen, took my hand, and led me to one of the tables, he looked different, almost like a stranger. He'd lost maybe thirty pounds, which made him seem even taller than his six feet two inches. He had grown a beard and his eyes were deeper, and darker, more intense. He seemed fragile somehow, beautiful even. I pushed at the glass of wine someone had placed in front of me, moving it a couple of inches away. I reminded myself not to be a fool and get drawn into loving Bill Bonanno again.

The last time I saw him, four months earlier and about half a year after he was released from prison the last time, Bill had called to tell me he wanted to come over for dinner and talk to me and the kids. We were living separately.

Since it was three days before Christmas, I pre-

pared a festive dinner. Afterward he said he had
something important to tell us. We left the dinner
table and went into the living room. I noticed that
he did not look at or mention the desk I'd moved
into the living room or the filing cabinet or the
appointment slips tacked to a bulletin board, all
signs that my career was thriving, something Bill
would ordinarily find hard to swallow. He waited
until we all settled into chairs, then sipped ice water
from a tumbler and said in his lawyerly way (a
manner of speaking he'd picked up serving as a
paralegal in his and his father's many legal battles),
"As you know, my life has been controlled by pris-
ons and courts for the last ten years. Grandma is
dead. Grandpa is going to prison. I don't know
what to do next. I have emotional and personal
problems. Due to some or all of these events in my
life, it's necessary for me to go away for a while
to get my head together."

It was true. Bill didn't look in the best of health,
and he was impossible to talk to or reason with. I
wondered if anyone else was after him now: the
FBI, some grand jury, or other men from his world.

"I can't tell you where I'm going, or how long
I'll be gone because I don't know myself. I won't
be in touch with anybody until I get back. I'm not
excluding you from anything. This is just the way
it is."

I watched the look on my children's faces,
knowing that I didn't care and wondering if they
did. Chuck and Joe and Tore, all young men now,
looked understanding if a little blank. What could

they ever say to their father anyway? Their only choice was to show respect and remain silent. My daughter, Gigi, my husband's favorite, the youngest of my children at sixteen, looked worried, but not surprised. Nobody said, "Hey, Dad, can't you at least wait till after Christmas?"

After that night he was gone: no phone calls, no word, no news. This was nothing unusual, really. My husband had been missing before. Bill was not your normal, everyday nine-to-five kind of husband, who goes off to a job, returns, eats dinner, watches television, goes to bed. My husband is the son of Joseph Bonanno, who the newspapers and the government say was the head of a Mafia family and that he was his father's *consigliere*. This, however, is not what my husband says. My husband says Mafia is a figment of the media's imagination. He says *mafia* is an adjective, not a noun. To be mafioso is to be brave and honorable. He says it means being a man, audacious but never arrogant. My husband says that he and his father are men of honor who do things according to the ethos of a 750-year-old tradition transported to the United States from Sicily. The Sicilian tradition has a system of respect, of kinship, a code of behavior that tells you what is right and what is wrong. According to this code people fight their own battles and have no need to go to outside authorities such as the police. My husband tells the story of a woman whose husband has just been killed. The police say, "But who did this?" And the woman replies, "It does not matter, as long as he knows," nodding to the baby boy she holds in her arms. That tradition is dying, thanks to the changing times. I have not raised the children to follow in their father's footsteps—to live staunchly within this tradition—as my husband was raised to follow in his father's.

Although my husband tells me my father, Salvatore Profaci, moved in the same world and was as much an adherent of the tradition as my husband—and that surely having been raised by Salvatore I must possess an inherent understanding of that world—the truth is I have a hard time with it. To me it means I can never ask questions, such as: Where are you going? How did you get the money? or How are we going to pay the rent, or the doctor bill, or the water tax? The life-style my husband leads, which I suppose is essential to his position within the Sicilian tradition, as it has been translated into the culture of the United States, means, as far as I can tell, that he does not go to a job, has lots of cash sometimes, and no money others. It means there were times he never left the house unless he was wearing a gun, and there were times when he had at least one guy in front of him and two guys in back wherever he went. *Bodyguards* is one word, I believe; *decoys* is another. My husband is constantly engaged physically, mentally, emotionally, and monetarily in court battles (it's said that old gangsters never die, they just become lawyers) and at one time fought in what the media called a gang war. What I knew about this gang war was nothing except that there were FBI men stationed outside my front door, questioning my

kids when they left for school; there were flood-
lights pointed at my house; and there were nights
when my husband didn't come home and then one
evening would break into his own house—unob-
served by the FBI, the police, or whomever else he
didn't want to see—blindfold me, and take me off
to a motel or an empty house or the backseat of a
car to make love. The blindfold was for my own
good. "It's for your protection. The less you know,
the better off you'll be," are words I have heard
often.

Bill's complex personality made him different
even within his world. I never knew anyone like
him. What the media doesn't know about or finds
too boring to tell, are the normal times. The days
when we're not dodging subpoenas. When my husband was home, he was home. But, really, even
then it wasn't normal; it was more like a situation
comedy, where every day is Saturday because
Dad's always there. I wanted Bill to get a job, use
his many talents. I wanted Bill to be different, to
answer the phone or the door, take out the garbage,
mow the lawn, or paint the bedroom. We had no
checkbook, no savings account, no life, health, or
car insurance. In fact, there were no plans. The way
people plan for a vacation, put money aside, and
make reservations—none of that. But one day my
husband might show up after being gone for a couple of weeks—while I was pinching pennies to
make whatever money he'd left me last—and say,
"Pack a bag. We're going to Haiti," and then guide
me through casinos, his hand on the small of my

back, people paying us homage like royalty.

I will say one thing: Life with my husband has been anything but boring. Our marriage has been written about. It is part of "Mafia" lore. I am Rosalie Profaci, eldest daughter of Salvatore Profaci, said to be the righthand man, the brains behind the brawn, of his brother Joe Profaci, the head of the Profaci family. When I married Bill it was said to be a marriage of a prince and a princess, the uniting of two powerful families. The problem was that I had no idea what I was getting myself into and Bill had no idea I had no idea. In other words, if I was a princess I didn't know it; and furthermore, even if I was a princess, I've been striving all my life to be a commoner while my husband has been striving to be a prince.

Last Christmas, when my husband left, I felt less than a commoner. I felt a fool. I counted the years we'd been married—almost twenty-five—and the years we'd been separated because my husband was either in jail or just not home—twelve years. I thought how I felt peaceful, in charge of my own life, when he was gone; how I felt almost normal. I'd made a career for myself. I had drive and ambition. I had a budget. I paid the mortgage, the gas, the electric. I had a checking account. I had insurance. I'd painted the fence around our house a dusky blue, and I'd planted trees and bushes. I was planning on owning my house and living in it for the rest of my life. My goal was to give my children stability. Mostly, though, I'd changed the way I looked at things, the way I was inside. I'd always

believed that God was my partner in life, but now
I felt him inside of me instead of up above and
separate; I felt like I had more choices; I felt less
a victim. I asked myself: What did God mean by
"What God has joined together, let no man put
asunder?" Did he really mean for me to remain in
a marriage that made me unhappy? I came to the
conclusion that if God forgives sins, he must forgive mistakes. In God's eyes, I was half-sure, divorce from my husband would not be a sin that
would result in my burning in hell.

But the fact remained that my husband, due to
his Old World ways, would never allow it. And
when the children were little I never would have
entertained the idea either, partly because I was a
different person then, but most certainly because
I'd lose my children. My husband always said,
"You leave with what you came with," meaning
only myself. My husband is a powerful man. He
would have somehow arranged it that there would
be no way I could live in this world unless it was
as his wife. I could go through all the legal channels, I could even get the divorce papers in my
hand, but there is no wall thick enough or high
enough, no country strong enough, to keep my husband from me, so certainly no piece of paper was
going to do it.

But my husband had seemed different the last
few years: sad, calm, a little distracted. His letters
from jail had become philosophical and bitter, as
though, because of something I'd done, there was
no way he could love me anymore. His mother had

died a few months before Christmas. His father had
been convicted of an obstruction of justice charge
and was facing prison at age seventy-eight; he
wasn't well and it was possible that he could die
there. My husband's world seemed to be shifting.
When my husband had left that evening before
Christmas, I'd even felt like embracing him, which
was not a feeling I'd had for some time. Family
and ritual have always been important to my husband, yet he was not spending Christmas with his
family. Maybe, finally, he would let me go. Maybe
we could go our separate ways. Maybe I could get
a divorce.

So, one brisk March morning I put on my dark
green suit, the one I save for important business,
and, accompanied by my lawyer, walked into the
Santa Clara County Courthouse and filed for divorce.

Three days later I got a phone call to go to the
Good Samaritan Hospital and wait for a call at a
public phone. It was a routine I'd grown accustomed to over the years because of government in-
trusions into our private lives. This time the reason
my husband had to be careful was because since
he'd left he'd been accused of committing grand
theft, a charge the government had been working
on since 1975. It was now 1981. The specter of yet
another court battle looming in the future had made
divorce all that more appealing. Also, the realization that my husband might be in hiding strength-
ened the possibility that I could actually get away
with a divorce, because if he returned he'd be ar-

rested. This gave me a false sense of security and autonomy.

When I picked up the phone, my husband did not say hello before he said, "You do not do this behind my back." His voice had that cold menacing commanding tone he used when there would be no discussion allowed. This was an order. "You do this to my face."

"I couldn't," I said, gathering all my courage, "I don't know where you are."

"I'm out of the country," he said. "If you think I won't come back there to stop you, no matter what goddamn court has what charge out against me, you're out of your mind. I've been making plans to come back anyway, and when I do I'll need ties to the community, a residence, to get bail. I don't need you running around up there causing trouble. You don't run out on me when I'm down. I want you to withdraw those papers."

"I can't."

"What do you mean, you can't? Nobody puts me into a corner, especially you. You do not divorce me. Divorce is not a thing you do. When we married, we married for life. Commitments are a promise to God, and to break them has serious consequences both in this life and the next."

He had softened his tone. It was turning my knees to jelly. I had to admit I agreed with him.

He said, "We've made it this long, Rosalie. After all we've been through. We can start over. We can make it work. You can't throw it away now. I need you."

I grew sadder and sadder, and more confused, and that was how I ended up withdrawing the divorce papers, and in Mexico with my husband on my birthday.

"Look at her, *mira, mira*," he said. "Forty-five years old and doesn't look a day past twenty-five." The Mexicans nodded deeply and smiled. The owner of the restaurant, Saro, another Sicilian, raised his glass and said, "To Rosalia."

Mexico was a bold and wild place. In the beginning, when we were still in a hotel room, screaming birds woke us every morning. We took long rides past craggy cliffs and strangled trees. Past hillsides shouting with color. We walked on the beach. We sat on rocks and stared at the waves, relentlessly approaching, crashing on rocks, spewing white spray as the seagulls jetted toward the sun, their cries splitting the air.

I wanted to like Mexico. But it was so wild: dead dogs and cows left on the side of the road, sidewalks begun and then abandoned when they ran into trees, storms bursting from the sky and shattering a previously peaceful afternoon. Nothing was planned. People lived in the moment. This country was a place where my husband could thrive, but it was not a place for me. I like order. Everything in its place. I like to plan. To know where I am so I know where I'm going. I wanted to leave but it was hard to get away. I had my work waiting. My daughter still in high school. I went home a couple of times to handle some of my customers, to put some things in order, to sell some jewelry so we could live on the money. I wanted to go home another time, but he wouldn't let me.

I said, "But Gigi needs me. I've got to check up on her. I can just imagine what she's eating. Nobody's there to make sure she goes to school every day."

"Gigi can take care of herself," he said. "She's sixteen years old. By that time I'd been on my own for years. She's got a town full of relatives up there. You're making excuses."

I pictured my daughter alone in the house. I imagined her eating peanut butter and jelly, or nothing at all. She'd told me everything was fine, but I still pictured her wandering from room to room, lost. Wondering how her mother could desert her. My son Joseph was taking state board tests for medical school, my son Tore was a freshman at San Diego State. They certainly could get by without me. Chuck, my oldest, worked in his mechanic shop and lived at home, but he probably never came home before midnight. My heart broke thinking of my daughter, so young and already alone in the world. I wondered if Gigi, never a school lover, was doing her homework. I wanted to talk to a counselor at her school. This was not right. A mother should be with her daughter.

I brought up my husband's favorite argument as my argument. "What about tradition? Is it traditional for a mother to leave her daughter?"

"It is traditional for a wife to be with her husband, to trust his decision, not to argue."

The last thing I felt for my husband was trust. Was he clinging to me so needfully now because of his situation: Because if he went back to the States he'd get arrested? Because he was in a foreign land alienated from most everything and everyone he knew? Was he being so attentive because he could feel I wasn't sure I wanted him anymore?

Sex was more sensual, erotic, and spontaneous in Mexico than it had ever been before. Yet it felt almost as though we were animals, as though the lovemaking had nothing to do with love, but with danger and fear and desperation. There were times when I was convinced there was no recovering the warm feelings, no way to rebuild the trust and the love I'd lost over the years, and still there were other times when I thought maybe it was possible to start over, to still love him.

I'd loved Bill since I was little. As children our families would gather during the summers or on Sunday afternoons, eating and drinking and laughing. The adults would grow silent whenever Bill's father spoke, showing Joseph Bonanno more respect than they showed anybody else. Off in the corners my cousins would tease me because everyone knew I was in love with his son Salvatore. Bill was the nickname he'd adopted when his family moved to Arizona for his health because Wild Bill was the rage for children those days. This American name had no doubt added to Bill's allure. That he was handsome, wore Western boots and shirts, and had such good manners might have been enough, but to top it off he was Sicilian and a friend of the family. I'd die for a chance to sit next to him. If he so much as looked at me I'd blush and picture that look for weeks.

But that tall, skinny boy had grown up and caused me so much pain in my life, emotional and spiritual, I was not even sure I respected him anymore. Especially when, as much as I tried not to, I found myself imagining some of the things he most certainly had done. During the time of the gang war, I'd passed a room in my own house and seen him and his father and their bodyguards and other men, men the newspapers would call his soldiers, holding glasses of brandy in the air, toasting, celebrating something. They were always meeting with each other. This life of his I did not understand, never had understood, and probably never would. Yet my husband has told me over and over that my father, whom I adored and respected more than any other human being, lived according to the same principles, the same code, and that he did what had to be done.

There was no denying that, regardless of all the pain, the disillusionment, the prison terms, the public and private humiliation, the times of neglect and no support—the fear—this man I'd been married to since I was twenty and whom I'd known all of my life was my life.

But still, I had to leave Mexico. I was not thinking of divorce now; I just knew I had to get back, to my home, my children, my life. I could not think straight when I was around Bill. He dominated me.

I had to get away from my husband to know what I felt.

I devised a plan of escape. This would not be the first time I'd tried to escape from him. He had taken my purse which had all my money and credit cards, but I had enough for a bus ticket to San Diego, where my son Tore was in college. If I could get that far, then I could borrow his car, or borrow money from someone, and make my way back home to San Jose.

On Sunday morning, when Bill went to buy a paper, I dressed in my bathing suit and took the beach bag in which I'd hidden my money and packed one change of clothing and a pair of shoes. The walk Bill would have to take to get the paper was a good twenty minutes. When he returned and found the house empty but nothing missing but my beach bag, he might think I just went for a swim, which would give me more time before he started to search for me. I walked quickly down the beach for at least a mile, then cut into town and to the bus station. I found out there would be no bus for an hour and a half. I had to change somewhere, and the one place I could think to go was the only hotel in town where Bill and I had never been together. It was a grand hotel where there were a lot of American tourists. My husband, who loves to eat almost as much as he loves for me to cook for him, probably never suggested we go there because someone might recognize him.

I bought a magazine and sat in the lobby. I couldn't concentrate on the words. I recalled the time I left him in Phoenix, when he was in the middle of his affair with a woman named Erica, when there was still no doubt in my mind that I loved my husband. He'd been living a double life. He had me in a house on the east side of town and Erica in a house on the west. He bought us both the same model and color of car—green Ford Falcons. I had my first two boys, Chuck and Joseph. She also had two sons. Before I'd met Erica I had no positive proof of his affair. Still, I knew in my bones he was in love with another woman. I even knew what she looked like. He gave me hints in his criticisms of me. He'd touch a certain part of my body and say, "You're so fat," or "You're so skinny," or "Why don't you bleach your hair?" or "How come you wear that kind of shoes?" By these hints I knew she was a blonde, with large breasts and narrow hips. I knew what sort of shoes she wore. I did not know how much my husband loved her or how much she loved him, but I guessed.

Finally, I'd had enough of the criticisms and the guessing. I called my mother in Brooklyn and asked her for money without telling her what for. If I had told her it was to leave my husband and go home to her, she would have refused to give it to me. She would have told me, as she had done before, "You do not run away. You tell him, and then if he agrees, and only if he agrees, do you leave." My mother was an old-fashioned woman, a Sicilian woman, of the belief that once you marry, you are your husband's property.

Didn't she know I could never tell my husband

I was leaving? He would not have allowed it. Hadn't she seen the bruise on my arm the last time I'd visited? Didn't she and the rest of my family know about my husband's temper? I could never have come out and said this to her. I was too ashamed.

I didn't tell her why I needed the money. I bought three tickets, one for me and each of my boys. Chuck was five and Joseph was three. We weren't in the sky for five minutes before the plane returned to make an emergency landing. I was sure that my husband had found me out and forced the plane down. By the time we landed, I was so hysterical I couldn't talk and could hardly walk. I was literally crippled with fear and in awe of the power my husband could wield. (Only later would I find out that the plane had had mechanical trouble that had nothing to do with my husband at all.) The stewardess held me by an elbow and led me off. Another stewardess had my boys. They brought us to a room in the airport where I confessed, because I thought they already knew, that my name was Rosalie Bonanno. My husband was Bill. They called him up. He came to the airport and brought me back home. We did not talk about the incident.

But that was long ago. Why was I so frightened now? It had been years since he'd laid a hand on me. I wasn't that scared girl anymore, heartbroken because my husband loved another woman, afraid of what would become of me out in the world without a man to support me. I had supported myself, had a career, made my own decisions. Why did I turn into such a scared, silent person with the posture of a cowering dog when around my husband? I began to pray to St. Christopher that I would have a safe journey. I prayed to the Sacred Heart to give me courage. I prayed that this time, God willing, I would make it back home. Then I would call Bill and apologize. Then we could reach a compromise. Then maybe he'd see that I couldn't just leave everything that was important to me to be with him.

When enough time had passed I walked back through the lobby and out the door. As I descended the steps, I saw him. He was sitting in the car looking at me. I felt my heart pound in my chest. I took a deep breath because I'd forgotten to breathe. He said, "Get in."

I froze.

He said, "Don't do this to me, Rosalie. Not now. Not when I need you."

I got in.

We did not talk. When he followed me into the cottage, he said, "What're we having for lunch?"

Neither of us spoke about my attempt to leave, and Bill seemed dejected. Certainly sad. In bed that night, I faced away from him and out the window. Perhaps it had been my fear that had drawn him to me. Perhaps I'd expected to be caught and so I was caught. I'd acted guilty when there was nothing to be guilty about. I decided I would not act guilty anymore.

The next morning, he told me we were going for

a ride. The sun was sharp and the air cool. He parked the car on a cliff and we climbed down some rocks to the beach. He stroked the back of my head, then put his hand on my neck. I could not stand the feel of his hands on me. I moved a foot away. "I have to leave, Bill," I said. "It's not because I want to leave you. I'll come back. But I have to at least ease my mind that Gigi's okay. Make sure everything's all right." I didn't dare mention my business reasons for returning. I knew how Bill would react to that.

He stared at the ocean and said nothing.

"I could bring warmer clothing, pans, my food mill, make this place more like a home."

"If you'd only learn," he said, shaking his head. "When you accept me and the way things are, there's a loosening of demands. When you fight and combat it, there's trouble. You are not a common person. You can't be a Nancy. You can't be a Beverly." (These were friends of mine with careers. Women who might talk back to their husbands, in public. Women who made their own decisions.)

I picked up a twig and began making roads in the sand.

"You're not accepting the reality of your situation," he said, "both before you married and after you married. You're still in a fantasy world and you're laying your own obstacles down. Nowhere is it written that life is fair."

"You wish I was a different person."

"Yes, I suppose I do."

And I wish you were a different person, I didn't say. Instead I interpreted what he was saying. My interpretation was this: Let it be his idea. Let him believe that I am not making any decisions on my own, and then I can get to do what I want. Sometimes.

When he pulled me into the sand and made love to me, I pretended at first to enjoy it, and then I did enjoy it. When we lay there, side by side, looking up at the sky, I said, "All I want is a little time. I just need to see that Gigi's as fine as she says. Check on the house. Bring some things down here to make the cottage more comfortable."

"Fine," he said. "All you had to do was talk to me."

I wondered.

Two days later, back in San Jose, I suspected Gigi was fairly happy to have me in Mexico. The house was not exactly spotless, but it wasn't a mess either. She'd made hamburger patties and put them in the freezer. There was a leftover roasted chicken in the refrigerator. Chuck had been giving her money for groceries and was home nearly every night for dinner now. She said she'd been baby-sitting and working at the department store. I asked her how she felt about my staying with her father.

She said, "Ma! Fine. I can't believe you. Don't worry. I'm fine. It was when you filed for divorce I wasn't fine. Why did you have children if you couldn't live up to your commitment?" Sometimes I think that of all my children my daughter is the one who most takes after the Bonannos. She has confidence and a strong sense of herself, as well as an innate and particular knowledge of what is right and what is wrong.

I knew she was right. I knew in my husband's way he was right too. It was just plain wrong to make a commitment, to make a promise before God, and then to try to break it.

My heart was lighter when I packed up my favorite pans. I bought a wheel of Romano cheese and packed my ceramic jar to keep it in once it was grated. I needed my food mill for the grinding of tomatoes. I took a pie tin, a cake pan, a tea kettle. I brought sheets and towels and rags to clean with. A radio.

It had been planned, just in case I was being followed by the FBI when I left San Jose for Mexico, that I would rent a car, meet my son Tore in San Diego, turn the car in, and then Tore would drive me back to Rosarito.

On the drive down I began to see a way it could work out with Bill. He had made good friends with Saro, who owned the Italian restaurant where we'd had my birthday party. Saro and Bill looked so much alike, people mistook them for brothers. Bill had taught Saro some of my dishes: pasta with broccoli sauce, fettuccine Alfredo, clam sauce, and marinara sauce. He'd taught Saro how to make them and Bill had cooked them himself in the kitchen many nights. Maybe they could be partners. Bill was happy in the restaurant. He was always at his best when he was being a host, surrounded by people, friendly and gregarious. Bill's personality would be good for business. He was content when he was busy, and running a restaurant would be a real job. Then I could get a job in San Diego; it was only minutes from the border. I could commute. In Mexico we could even have a bank account, a checkbook. There would be no IRS, no FBI, no criminal record, no publicity, no tapped phones. Our children were grown. They'd visit on holidays. Bill and I could have a new life.

A second chance.

I'd made plans with Tore to meet him at the airport, where I would turn in the rented car. When I arrived he was not at the appointed gate. I waited and waited. Finally, at midnight, I had him paged. His name is Salvatore Bonanno, the same as my husband's.

Tore had been at the west gate instead of the east.

He helped me take all the stuff from my car and load it into his, then we drove to our cottage. In the morning we unloaded the car and Tore drove back because he had to study for midterms.

I felt wonderful. After twenty-five years, Bill finally wanted what I wanted: a normal life. I felt at home for the first time in this strange country. Seeing my stuff all over the kitchen, knowing there was a turkey, imported pasta, and Romano cheese in the refrigerator, was comforting. I was sweaty after traveling, so I undressed to take a shower, and as I stepped under the steaming water, I looked out the window as was my unconscious custom. Only this time, instead of some dogs on the street and some birds flitting from tree to tree, I saw maybe a half dozen Mexican men in uniform surrounding our house. I shut off the water, tiptoed out of the bathroom, and called to Bill in a loud whisper. "There are men." Just as I said this there was banging on the door and a loud voice calling, "Mexican Judicial Police."

"Tell them you're in the shower. Tell them to wait a minute," Bill said. "I knew it. The goddamn FBI were at the airport."

Had it been my fault because I'd had them page Bill's name?

I said, "I'm showering, can you wait?" then ran into my room to put a bathing suit on under my towel while Bill moved into the hallway, which you could not see from the front room. I went to the door wrapped in the towel with my hair wet. I am not a good liar and never have been, but still I told them as convincingly as I could that my husband was not home.

Meanwhile, some other police had gone around to the back of the house and through a window had spotted Bill standing in the hallway, who in turn had spotted them. "Forget it, Rosalie," he said, walking into the living room.

The Mexican police stormed past me and threw Bill onto the floor. Two men, one on each side of him, held a gun to Bill's head, while another hand-cuffed his hands behind his back.

I sat on the sofa and covered my eyes.

The last thing I saw was Bill being shoved onto

the floor of a van. The last thing I heard was Bill calling, "Rosalie, I love you."

I must have wept for two days. I didn't know what to do. Was I supposed to stay and wait, or was it all right to leave? I finally got word from Bill's cousin Jack that Bill had been brought to the border and arrested by the FBI. He was being held in Alameda County on a grand-theft charge with a bail of one million dollars. I knew that Bill had had to borrow money to live on for the past months. How would he ever make bail? I was afraid he would ask his aunt to sell the house and borrow the money from her; or even ask her to put the house up for bail! But then, Aunt Marion was a widow and was not well. She had decided to stay on the East Coast near things she knew. Would I lose the house we had made into a home? When his lawyer called one morning and asked if I'd appear at a bail-reduction hearing, I lost it. I began to shout, "I will NEVER sit in another courtroom and answer another question to get my husband out of ANYTHING!"

When I hung up I was shaking. After I calmed down a little, I began to wonder, not for the first time, how Rosalie Profaci, the shy little girl from Brooklyn—the one who was going to have a good life because she never committed any sins, the one who always did what she was told, never asked questions, and never talked back, especially to a man, no less a lawyer, the one who thought she had married a cowboy who would take her away to a new and different life—ever grew up to bow her head before news cameras and to pack picnics for her children, not to eat under the shade of a tree in the country but in the car on the long drive to visit their father in prison.

CHAPTER 2

I can't remember a time before I knew Bill. He'd been around all my life because our fathers were not only friends but allies in their world. When my father arrived in Canada from Sicily in 1926, his brother Joseph called Stephen Magaddino in Buffalo and asked him to arrange for my father to cross the border. Canada was a main source of illicit liquor at the time, and illicit liquor being a staple of my uncle Joseph's and Stephen Magaddino's incomes, I suppose arrangements for bringing my father into the United States from Canada were not difficult to make. It was Joseph Bonanno, Stephen Magaddino's cousin, who was sent to Canada to ease my father's way.

When Mr. Bonanno met my father, they were both young men in their early twenties. They did not go directly back to New York, but spent a couple of months living and working together at bootlegging in Buffalo, so that by the time Mr. Bonanno delivered Joe Profaci's little brother to him, not only had a friendship been forged, but a lasting alliance in their world. This was nothing official, just a recognition of similar sensibilities, of a similarity of personality and the approach to the way they did things. They palled around before they married, going to shows, looking for women, frequenting clubs. They became *compares:* My father was an usher in Bill's father's wedding and Bill's parents were my sister's baptismal godparents, and his mother was sponsor at my confirmation.

And so when there was a large gathering of family and friends, the Bonannos as often as not were present, and so was their son Bill, who my great-grandmother named *cetriòlo*, which means cucumber, because he was so tall and thin. These gatherings were often at a farm in the country, which leaders in our fathers' worlds had bought because they could list the men who worked for them as farmworkers and in that way render them ineligible for the draft. I would stare shamelessly at Bill, not because I was bold, far from it, but because I was so enamored I forgot myself.

He was four years older than I was, and so tall, and so handsome, and so American, I was smitten. He lived in Arizona, wore western clothes, did not speak with a Brooklyn accent, and was treated more like a man by my father and my uncle than my brothers and cousins were.

He had a quick smile and an easy laugh, an open, friendly manner, which was foreign in my world, where people were distrustful and guarded and where the boys were always eager to show respect and anticipate what their fathers wanted. It's not that Bill did not show respect; he just did it without showing fear.

Bill rode horses, worked on cattle ranches, and brought cattle from Mexico on cattle trails. He worked as a wrangler at dude ranches and taught Easterners not to be afraid of the world he loved so much. He hunted for wild boar. He flew airplanes. At fourteen he had his own car and at sixteen he'd driven across country. He was better than a Prince Charming or a knight in shining armor; for a Sicilian girl in Brooklyn in the 1940s and 1950s, there was nothing quite so romantic as a cowboy. In fact, I had a picture of Bill on a horse that I carried around in my wallet and showed to anybody who was interested, presenting him as my boyfriend, when I doubt that he'd even noticed me as being anything more than one of a pack of Profacis.

Every summer my younger sister, Annie; my older brother, Sal; my younger brother, Frank; and I spent weeks and sometimes as long as a month with my six Profaci boy cousins and two Profaci girl cousins at their father's, my uncle Joe Profaci's, farm in New Jersey. The farm was a forty-acre estate that had once belonged to Teddy Roosevelt. The house had thirty rooms, and there was a chapel with an altar that was a hand-carved replica of St. Peter's Basilica in Rome. The Bonannos were often guests there too. When they were, it was Bill who played the negotiator between the kids and the adults, gaining us girls permission to drive into town with the boys to buy ice cream or go to the movies. As long as Bill was driving it was fine for us to go along, but if it were one of the other boy cousins, then it was not. The boys and girls were fairly well separated usually: the boys went off to explore the grounds, rode the Jeep out to the pit to throw out the garbage, or to town for supplies. They cleaned the pool by emptying it and scrubbing it like a bathtub because it had no filtering system, while we girls stuck close to the house to help Aunt Fifi gather the laundry and towels, wash and hang them out properly, then fold them carefully in preparation for ironing. The two ironing boards were always in use because dish towels, underwear, and socks as well as shirts had to be ironed perfectly. My aunt was the orchestrator of the farm and zealous about cleanliness. I was usually stationed at one of the sinks or stoves helping my cousins make apple pies (when apples started to ripen at the end of the summer), and cheesecakes which we learned to love when we went to Lindy's restaurant after the plays in New York.

There's a story about Aunt Fifi that we liked to laugh about. There was an article in a newspaper about how the police had come to Uncle Joe's house in Brooklyn, and they quoted Aunt Fifi as yelling, "Cheez it! It's the cops!" which never in a million years would have happened. If Aunt Fifi had said anything, it would have been in Italian, and it would've been, "Watch where you put your hands."

There was a lot of emphasis put on food at the farm. The amount and quality of food served in a Sicilian home represents the generosity and success

of the breadwinner, and my uncle Joe was not only
an important man but had a big appetite. There was
a room with nothing but vegetables in it, and a
freezer filled with ice cream. We girls helped Aunt
Fifi prepare institutional-sized breakfasts where
everybody lined up with a plate and we shoveled
two eggs, several strips of bacon, and two pieces
of toast on each. Uncle Joe bought whole salamis,
and we'd lay one loaf of bread on the table for the
bottom layer of a sandwich, load the salami on,
then some cheese, and cover it with another loaf.

In the evening or on weekends when the adults
were around, there were great vats of pasta, bottles
of wine, and much laughter. It didn't escape me
that everyone listened a little more attentively when
Mr. Bonanno spoke. My family respected him and
perhaps held him in a little bit of awe. He was well-
read and well educated, in addition to possessing
the gift of a good storyteller. To say that Mr. Bonanno was the only one among them who was well
educated, though, is not to say he was the only
intelligent man.

My father was a successful businessman who
owned two clothing factories that worked round the
clock to make uniforms for the armed services during the war, then raincoats afterward; a high-
fashion shoe factory that counted movie stars
among its clientele; and extensive real estate holdings. According to my husband, in the world they
came to share, my father was a very innovative
businessman who devised ways of keeping track of
a vast betting and numbers business, and was a

cool-headed manager who knew how to keep my uncle's boisterousness and temper in line. My uncle was a flamboyant man who smoked big cigars, drove big black Cadillacs, and did things like buy tickets to a Broadway play for us cousins. But he didn't buy two or three or even four or five seats, he bought a whole row. I remember one time when, in an uncharacteristic gesture, my father acted like his brother. He walked into a room where we cousins were celebrating the New Year and threw fistfuls of dollars in the air, then laughed as he watched us dive for the bills. Normally, in personality, my father was the opposite of his brother. He abhorred ostentatious shows of wealth, and was reserved and level-headed. And, so it is said, my father was the brains behind the brawn, the cool-headed businessman who kept everybody's tempers in check and the profits rolling in.

I was in love with my father. He was a mild, introspective, and quiet man who wore glasses and had a shock of thick black curly hair that he suffered me to brush this way and that when I was little. My father didn't know how to read or write in English, and I remember being around eight or nine and sitting at the dining-room table filling out some government contract forms for him in my third-grade printing. When we were done he put his hand on my shoulder and smiled at me, and I knew he was very proud to have a daughter so young who could read and write, and in English. I imagine my father felt inadequate because of his own lack of education, and it was very important for him to make something of himself in this country and to provide his children with the best education. My parents sent my brothers to the New York Military Academy, and, trying to do for me as the aristocrats in Italy had done for their daughters, they sent me to an exclusive convent school, Mount St. Mary's, upstate in Newburgh, New York. It was far from Brooklyn and my insular family, but in the same town as my father's factories and next to Cornwall, where we had our summer home.

I was only six years old when they sent me to Mount St. Mary's and was frightened and terribly lonely and confused at first, but then the austere beauty of that school, the white marble interiors, the rolling green lawns, and the kindness and nurturing of the nuns began to work its spell and I was absorbed into a comfortable life of ritual and conformity. I loved to walk to the grottoes and sit alone by the statues. I wondered if I would see these saints if I made it into heaven. That first year when I was chosen to lead the May procession and crown a statue of the Blessed Mother, I took it as a sign of grace. I proudly wore a white dress and strutted along, keeping an eye on Sister Imelda Marie who walked to the side of the procession and encouraged me. Then I came to the scary part. I had to climb a ladder by myself, then place a wreath of flowers on Mary's head. When I did this, I felt special and sure that I'd be rewarded with a special place in heaven. I was also sure that if I was good, all good things would come to me in life.

For some reason, perhaps prophetic, I was very worried about my family. Was there a mysterious side to my father that seemed bad? I prayed every day to the Sacred Heart to protect them and care for them and not to let harm come to them. I loved the rhythm of the rituals, of mass every morning, Benediction every Thursday, confession every Saturday, and communion every Sunday. Lent was my favorite season. Then I'd give up whatever I loved the most that year and offer it up to God. On Holy Week I went to church on Holy Thursday, Good Friday, and Holy Saturday. I think Holy Thursday was my favorite because on this day we read the entire life of Christ and celebrated the Last Supper when he gave us His body and blood for remembrance. The breaking of bread was a symbol of communication among humanity. Later when I had children, I'd insist that everyone be present for dinner on Holy Thursday so we could break bread.

My school training was the beginning of an abiding and strong love of God that has gone through many changes but has never failed to help me by giving me strength, comfort, and at times even wisdom. Still, as enamored as I was with the life at Mount St. Mary's, as lost to the world as I could get during masses, or while sketching the stained-glass windows in chapel, sneaking peeks into the nuns' quarters to see if they had hair, or practicing the piano, I was ecstatic to see my father's green Pontiac pull up the drive. It never oc-

curred to me that my father was different from the
other fathers who visited, even though my father
never dressed up like the South American million-
aire fathers of other girls. When he visited on Saturdays, he wore his workman's trousers with a rope
for a belt. My father was not only excessively modest but also frugal. If he had to entertain people
from Washington for his business, he did it at our
small house perched on the side of a mountain in
the country, and he served them good Italian food
my mother prepared, on a picnic table that was so
crooked a wine bottle laid on its side would roll
right off.

My husband likes to say that I was not educated
correctly by my father. Bill had assumed he was
marrying a girl who would need no training for her
position in life as his wife, who would not be upset
when her husband didn't come home and then
didn't tell her where he'd been; a woman who
would trust always that whatever her husband did
was for the better, and so she would have no de-
sires or needs to contribute to decision-making, or,
for that matter, to make her own decisions. My husband believed he was marrying a young woman
schooled in the old-country Sicilian tradition, and
he assumed that my father had taught me a thing
or two about what that meant.

My father was a retiring man, not one for making speeches, giving lectures, or imparting old-
world sayings and wisdom, but he did teach us
some things. He told us children that we were different from "them," meaning Americans: We were

clean, we worked hard, we never lied, and we never
cheated. We respected our elders, acted like ladies
and gentlemen, and avoided the wickedness in the
world. And we did things differently. I did not
smoke or drink or swear or even wear slacks. I did
not go to games at the neighboring New York Military Academy, nor did I go on dates. It was as
though there were an invisible fence separating me
and my family from the rest of the world. I was
not allowed to leave the house unless I had a des-
tination, and then I could go only if I was accompanied by one of my brothers or a cousin. In
Brooklyn when we would pass the other kids playing on their stoops or hanging out on a corner, I
would wonder what it was like to be them, to be
so loose and undisciplined, so free and unprotected.
I know at least some of them thought I was stuck
up because it was what they most liked to yell in
my direction as I walked past.

My father's protectiveness, the insularity of my
whole world, made me feel special, and at the same
time made me feel different in not such a wonderful way. I was aware that my parents were immi-
grants and that I didn't share the same cultural
references as other children my age. I didn't know
pop songs or have crushes on movie stars, and I
suppose I would have liked to have more of a feeling of belonging, of blending in. Even though I was
told that I was "better," I was also made to feel
that what I had to say was, almost without excep-
tion, of no consequence or import. For my brothers

or any of the boys it was different. What they had
to say mattered.

Between the seventh grade and high school I left
Mount St. Mary's for a spell to attend a school in
Brooklyn called Visitation Academy, where I was
taught by cloistered nuns, who never spoke unless
they were teaching and never stepped foot outside
the walls of their convent. At Visitation we wore
hats and gloves to school and had classes in eti-
quette and letter writing. A bell clanged to signal
the end of a class, and when our parents came to
talk to the nuns, they did so at a small window in
the wall where they had to speak through an iron
grating. As far as my parents were concerned, I was
getting an excellent education. I was to learn to
speak French and to play the violin and to set a
table properly and to have no other ambitions than
to be a good wife and mother. This was fine with
me. I knew no different. It was my dream to have
a wonderful family and a rich, joyful, and pious
home life. I was also taught by my parents and the
nuns that I was to do as my parents said and then
as my husband said. I was trained to be the kind
of girl who would not give a man any problems.
Since no one wanted to hear what I had to say, I
was silent around my father and other men. Men
were simply more important. As a family, we
would not eat until my father came home, and then
my mother waited on him hand and foot.

The only date I was ever allowed to go on was
to my brother's senior prom with a friend of his,
and only because my brother was going with us.

This is not to say that I didn't like boys and didn't
flirt with the boys my brother brought home from
the Academy. When I was in high school, we
moved permanently to Cornwall and I became a
day student at Mount St. Mary's. My brothers were
day students at the Academy, and we all had
friends over after school.

One time, when my father was out of town, a
girlfriend of mine arranged a date for me to a West
Point prom. This was no small thing. In fact, in my
social circle at Mount St. Mary's, this was considered an honor, so I convinced my mother to let me
go, which was not too difficult. My mother was ten
years younger than my father and only twenty years
older than me. At times she seemed more like one
of us kids than a parent. This impression was
heightened by the fact that she rarely had any
money of her own. She had to ask my father for
whatever she needed as well as beg his permission
if she wanted to buy or do anything. Whenever
there was a punishment to be meted out, she de-
ferred to my father by saying, "Wait till your father
gets home." She was a heavy woman with a big
bosom, who dressed in flowered house dresses and
sensible shoes. She had a wonderful sense of humor and a very warm heart. Even though she knew
my father would object to my dating, she thought
that maybe just this once there would be no harm.
But my father happened to come home unexpect-
edly that same evening, and when he heard about
my plans he was livid. He said absolutely no, there
would be no date for his daughter. When I went

into my room to change out of my dress and collapsed on my bed, I realized I was actually more
relieved than sad. I was a shy girl who took pride
in being pious and religious, did not like doing anything wrong ever, and had only convinced my
mother to let me go on this date in the first place
because I'd been so pressured by my girlfriends.
But then I wondered how the cadet would take to
missing his prom. I wondered if he'd take the re-
jection personally or if he'd understand about strict
fathers. This made me feel guilty and very sad for
him.

I never resented the restrictions imposed upon me
by my father. That's just the way it was in our
family and I was not the type of girl who rebelled
or questioned authority. My younger sister Annie
was different. To a certain extent, because she was
bolder, she got away with things I would never dare
attempt, such as visiting the houses of friends after
school, and voicing her opinion at dinner. Yet even
though she did not share my docile and accepting
nature, she, like me, hardly noticed and definitely
did not question the fact that squares of text were
often cut out of the newspaper before we read it.
Perhaps there was a family taboo against such
questioning. Nor did I ask how it was that when a
crown of jewels that rested above Mary's head at
Regina Paci, a local church, was stolen, my uncle
arranged for its return; or why at my uncle's farm
there were so many guard dogs, and strange men
who were never invited to sit down to eat with

everyone else but who hovered near doorways or stood around outside along the drive.

There was a woman named Pearl who was often a guest at family gatherings with her daughter. She liked to talk to the men more than to the women, and everybody knew she was looking for a nice Profaci boy for her daughter. She was funny and boisterous and everyone liked her. The thing that I might have thought strange about Pearl was that her husband had been shot to death beside her in a car and that Pearl, although she lived through the assassination, ended up with two bullet holes in her belly, which she would show to us children if we begged her. It did not seem particularly odd to me that my family was friends with a woman with holes in her belly and a gunned-down husband. Nor did it seem odd to me that at my graduation party— attended by one hundred people at a hotel in Cornwall—I received a lavish gold bracelet and a diamond watch from friends of my father's whom I did not know. My father had rented some upstairs rooms, where the men all met with each other, and other men stood along the hallway keeping watch or waiting to be called inside the room.

I had an excuse for lack of curiosity at my party, though. It was my high school graduation, after all, and I did have other things on my mind, not the least of which was Bill Bonanno. Bill, who was a sophomore at a college in Arizona and a member of the ROTC, had finally taken notice of me. It had happened the summer before when his family came to visit us, and then Bill and I rode to Albany with his parents. The two of us sat in the backseat together and laughed and talked. He told me how he planned to be a lawyer and how much he wanted a pilot's license. I could see in his eyes during that ride that it was different, that he wasn't looking at me like I was a little girl. But neither was I so deluded as to believe I was very important to him. I was forever hearing rumors of his having many girlfriends—Americans, college students, fast girls who drove cars and smoked cigarettes, and who probably swore and were not even Catholic.

Then, that winter, in 1953, my father sent me and my brother out to Arizona for a visit. The ride was thirteen hours long. The plane stopped eight times. I felt as though I were traveling to a foreign country, and it wasn't only because of the time it took to get there. The sky was huge. The mountains were ominous and thrilling; they changed colors with the position of the sun and the passing of a cloud. I had fantasized that Bill would spend every minute with me and that at the end of my visit he'd declare his undying love and it would be only a matter of graduating from high school before we married and I moved out to this wild land. But, as so often happens, my fantasy did not match the reality. Bill was very busy with his life. He went off to meet friends and attended classes, which made me mortally disappointed that he wasn't spending every minute with me. Yet when we said good-bye at the airport, he did kiss me and squeeze my hand. Neither of us had said any words about it, but we both had a definite sense that our fathers would be very happy if we fell in love. For Bill, that was a possibility he was going to consider. I was already sure because I'd been in love with him since I was ten.

It was at my graduation, though, that I was sure Bill was more interested in me than in the other girls who flocked around him. I was the only girl he danced with, and when I was talking with friends or dancing with another boy I could feel his eyes on me. When we parted at the end of the evening, he told me that he had to get back to Arizona for ROTC camp but that he would write to me. When he shook hands with my father, he said he'd be back at the end of the summer and my father invited Bill to go fishing on his boat with him. There seemed a subtle difference in the relationship between Bill and my father that I couldn't put my finger on. It was as though there was nothing left of a man talking to a boy in my father's attitude toward him.

I wouldn't know until many years later that something had happened to Bill a few months before my graduation, some sort of ceremony or celebration where people gave him presents, one of which was a four-carat diamond pinkie ring. This ceremony somehow initiated him into my father's world, where he was to hold a position of respect. The only thing I would know was what Bill said to me before we married, that he was already married to something else—a statement I regretfully did not understand or question.

• • •

My father suffered from severe hay fever, and during the summers would spend a month out on his boat on the ocean, often taking us along with him. I loved to cook for him and his friends in the tiny galley and to eat in the sun with the taste of salt on my lips.

Two months after my graduation we were in Cornwall and Papa had gone on his annual hay fever trip off the New Jersey shore when my mother took a call from my uncle. She hung up the phone, closed her eyes, then snapped back to life in an instant. She called all of us to her. Sal was nineteen, I was eighteen, Frank seventeen, Annie thirteen, and my baby sister Victoria seven.

"Sal," she said, "do you think you can drive all the way to New Jersey?"

"Sure," he said.

"No time for complaints. Everyone in the car," she commanded as she rounded us out the door.

In the car she told us about the terrible accident.

One of my father's engines had exploded and my father had been thrown from his boat. A woman, whom my father had just left on the dock with a group of other guests, dived into the water and rescued him, but he was seriously burned.

When we finally got to see my father in the hospital, he was in a tent and his body was covered with a rubber sheet that was strewn with ice. He had third-degree burns over three quarters of his body. I remember looking at his thick hair, which had not been singed, and thinking how beautiful it was, even more so now that it was salt and pepper. Finally, I summoned the courage to look from his hair to his eyes. What I saw in my father's eyes I had never seen there before. It was fear. More than anything, I wanted to reach out to him, to stroke his hair, to say, "Papa, please don't be scared." I wanted to tell him to pray, to ask for forgiveness, but I didn't have the courage because I didn't want him to think I thought he was dying.

For two weeks he straddled a thin line between life and death. Speaking was a terrible strain for him and the only words I heard him utter were endearments such as "baby doll" and "honey," which I suppose were his way of trying to give me comfort and to make me feel more brave. Every day, as I sat with my father, I thought the same thing: that more than anything I wanted to pray with him because I wanted to make sure his soul would be saved. I repeated over and over to myself, "Papa, let's pray," but I just could not make the words come out of my mouth. Finally, one afternoon, as we stood up to leave, with a tremendous strain he said, "My dollie." Those were the last words I ever heard my father say, and I never did tell him to pray.

The next day before we left the farm for the hospital my uncle walked in with a horrible look on his face, and we knew. We all embraced my mother and stood huddled like that for a while, crying and screaming. Then Aunt Fifi, who had made a big pot of lentil soup, insisted we eat. It was four in the afternoon, yet we sat down and ate—my mother, my two sisters and two brothers, all the cousins, my aunt and uncle, everybody.

I slept that night with my mother in the double bed my father and she shared when we stayed at my uncle's. My mother kept tugging at the sheet, pulling and pulling it between her hands. We never slept. My mother had gone to bed like she was supposed to. She didn't want to cause any commotion. If she cried she did it in the bathroom behind closed doors.

The wake and funeral were in Brooklyn. We sat at the funeral home from morning until night. Thousands of people came. They had to keep opening more rooms to accommodate the huge crosses and hearts and chairs done in flowers and lined up three rows deep. Their scent was overpowering and sickening. Five limos brought flowers to the graveyard. Twelve more brought people. People massed on the steps of the church and on the street. They screamed, "Turiddu, Turiddu," my father's name in Sicilian, as the hearse went by. Newspaper reporters, television cameras, throngs of people crowded the cemetery. I didn't understand the fuss. I'd known my father was an important man—he had three businesses and he employed a lot of people—but I had no idea he was *that* well liked and respected. But, then, I had nothing else to compare it with, so I didn't make too much of all the fuss. In fact, my father's funeral would be one of the last big funerals for people from his world, because soon it would be a different world, closely surveilled by the FBI and wary of publicity.

The nicest thing anyone said to me as I sat at
the wake with my family receiving condolences
was by a woman who worked in one of my father's
factories. Maybe it was as much the sincerity with
which she said it as it was the actual words. She
said, "Your father was a good man." Another
woman destroyed me. She said, "Ah, in a couple
of years you'll get married, have your own family.
You'll forget so fast."

I did get married, I did have a family, but I have
never forgotten, and to this day I find it impossible
to believe that my father was some kind of dangerous "gangster" or "mobster," or that he did anything more than run his factories, paint his boat,
and maybe run a few numbers operations.

CHAPTER 3

BILL wrote me a few kind, comforting letters after my father died. The following summer, he came up to Cornwall for a visit and things proceeded from there. For a Sicilian girl of my generation, brought up by a family with a will to keep the old traditions intact, there was no such thing as "dating," so from the first moment he took my hand as we strolled along the edge of our lawn—a gesture that infuriated my mother, causing her to accuse me of "flaunting"—we began to talk about the future and gauge whether we had similar enough ideals and dreams to get married.

By the time Bill returned to Arizona a month after he'd arrived, we'd kissed in the corner of my porch at night when everyone else was inside because of mosquitoes, we'd joked and laughed, and there was no question that we'd make a perfect match. We were both religious, intellectual, and idealistic. We agreed that marriage was an absolute, a vow before God, never to be broken. We both wanted children and thought that family was the point of it all, the bedrock of life. I told him about the time when I was maybe ten and had seen Jesus floating above the streetlight outside my window in

Brooklyn, and how honored I'd felt but also secretly disappointed, because deep in my heart I didn't want to be a saint. I wanted to be a wife and a mother. We laughed about that and then he put his arm around me and pulled me closer. This felt right to me, somehow preordained, that I would love Bill Bonanno with all my heart and soul, that I would share my life with him, and that he would be the father of my children. By the time Bill left for Arizona at the end of the summer we'd said "I love you" to each other, and I knew that very soon he would ask the big question.

I didn't have to wait long. Four days after he left I received his proposal in a letter, in which he warned me that if the answer was yes, I should say nothing to anyone before he was able to return and do what was proper. By this he meant that he'd first have to ask permission of my brother, who at nineteen had become the new head of my family, and then of my mother. He'd also have to ask my uncle Joe, who was now the official guardian of us all.

It touched me that Bill was so old-fashioned and respecting of tradition and genuinely concerned about doing the right thing, at the same time he was a modern cowboy way out West, going to college and planning to be a lawyer. He also seemed to respect me and my entitlement to my own opinions more than the other men I'd known. He was interested in what I thought, and encouraged me to talk. I believed I would be a true partner in his life. I thought I might be the luckiest girl on earth. His was a good family. The best. Mr. Bonanno had traveled through Europe, spoke French, and could converse about the arts or history or world affairs. It seemed to me he stood out among men, even my uncles. I imagined my father happy and proud that his daughter Rosalie would be wed to the son of his old friend, his first friend in this country, Joseph Bonanno.

I was too excited to wait the couple of weeks for Bill to return and make everything official. I ran downstairs and told my mother that I thought Bill and I would probably get married. She did not seem thrilled. She said, "We know his family but we don't know him. Isn't he a little wild for you, too experienced? You don't know how many girls he's had. Didn't your cousin Millie say something about a girl in California? And then we heard about some Rose from Pittsburgh, remember?"

I did remember—although before my mother brought it up I'd chosen not to—and I wrote directly to Bill because I believed that premarital sex was a sin and I did not want to marry a man who had committed it. Bill responded that he certainly had dated in his lifetime, but had never felt about any of these girls as he felt for me. And certainly there had been nothing "serious." I took this as an avowal of chastity and believed him absolutely.

When Bill returned to talk to my mother and my brother a few weeks later, I was sitting on the patio overlooking the mountains, crocheting, while they talked in the living room. When they walked onto the patio they were beaming, and it was all I could do to keep myself from blurting out, "So, when do I get the ring?"

I'd been dreaming of and preparing for this marriage, it seemed, my whole life. Sister Mary Consilia had an entire course on marriage, in which she taught us what to expect and how to behave. She'd told us that men admired femininity at all times, and since assertiveness and anger were not feminine, they were highly discouraged. Men would make the decisions and it was our duty to have faith in these decisions and to support them. A woman was to keep her body desirable for her husband only, and her home clean. I was to make do with what my husband brought home and should not desire luxuries, but if my husband could not provide me with the necessities, I should never complain and should be prepared to earn a living to help out. All of this I took to heart as I reviewed my notes, and I had no doubt that I'd live up to the nuns' expectations. They were not so divergent from the examples my mother and aunts had set for me. I began another notebook in which I jotted down my mother's recipes as I sat in the kitchen night after night watching her deftly throw together delicious pasta sauces. I dreamed of the day I'd have my own kitchen, and took much pride in keeping my mother's house spotless and the floors polished to a gleam.

I wasn't present when Bill told my uncle Joe, but apparently my uncle was thrilled, because within weeks he'd organized a big party at a restaurant in

Brooklyn, inviting two hundred relatives and *compares* and children of *compares* on both sides to make the announcement—this being traditional. But before that celebration, there was a smaller, more intimate meeting of the immediate family in Uncle Joe's living room—also traditional—where he sat on a thronelike chair with Bill next to him and asked everyone in the room whether or not they approved of our courtship. When he came to my sister Annie, who was fourteen and the rebellious one in the family, she shrugged her shoulders and said, "If she loves him then she should marry him."

My uncle grinned, nodded, and said, "In a few more years we'll find a husband for you."

Annie answered stridently, "I'll find my own husband," then my uncle turned red and puffed up and bit his finger. His anger came from the belief that women do as their families say and then do as their husbands say. Women did not have opinions, minds of their own, or any control or say in anything, including their own lives.

I didn't think my future husband thought like this. How could he? He was too American. It was true that it had been important to Bill that we do everything by the letter, to keep the old tradition, but we'd also done some things behind everyone's back. We had kissed and he'd proposed before we'd put the question to my family. But we had never gone and continued not to go out alone. When we went to the Latin Quarter or to other fine restaurants we were accompanied by my cousins or

Bill's friends. I collected sugar cubes from these restaurants, and before I married I had shoeboxes full. But often Bill and I just went for a ride and took my little sister Victoria along as a chaperone. When she fell asleep we threw a blanket over her in the backseat and then we parked. Our lovemaking never went further than kissing. Bill was very disciplined and determined not to betray the trust my uncle had put in him—a trust I had no idea was involved with much more than Bill's dating Salvatore Profaci's daughter. It had to do with the position they both held in that other world, a position that made Bill my uncle's equal in a sense. I, on the other hand, wished Bill might have been a little more persistent. I knew Bill had been taught all his life that there was a type of girl you used and a type you married, but Bill was so careful to keep his distance that I began to feel untouchable. I'd been taught by the nuns that men were more animalistic than women by nature and it was a woman's responsibility not to tease or tempt men by wearing low-cut dresses or tight pants, but I was eager to see more of Bill's "animal" nature. And certainly eager for my wedding night, because the nuns had also taught us that when a woman gives herself to a man in marriage, her body becomes his to do with as he will. There is no limit to our ecstasy, and this ecstasy is our only hint of heaven on earth.

All the fuss about our seeing each other had been made early in the fall, but it wasn't until January 1, 1956, that I got my five-carat diamond ring and had the official engagement party. I suppose I'd made a bit of a nuisance of myself before, asking for a ring to show to my girlfriends, many of whom had friendship rings from boyfriends. I must not have been very good at hiding my eagerness because my uncle Joe once took me aside and presented me with a parable, which he was fond of doing. He said, "An old man follows another old man around for years and years, his whole life, because he wants to know what the other old man has in his pockets. One day the old man who has been followed empties his pockets and shows the other old man all the contents; suddenly the man who's been following for years loses interest and never follows again."

I didn't listen to my uncle's old-world wisdom and continued to be candid about my feelings and to write Bill twice as many letters as he wrote me, because I thought that to act hard to get would be false and a sin. I wanted to be honest about who I was so Bill could decide before the big day if I was really his type of girl. I resented my uncle's giving me advice because it seemed to me that since my father died he was trying to take my father's place, first by convincing my mother to move from Cornwall to the house directly behind his in Brooklyn so that he could keep an eye out for us and then by creating a doorway through our common brick garage wall. He had also insisted that he should be the one to give me away at my wedding, while I insisted it must be my brother. Thanks to my mother's standing up to him, which took more than a little courage, I got my wish.

When I look back on it now, I realize I was proud to follow the Sicilian tradition in some ways, and in other ways I thought of myself as modern and was proud of this too. I was in conflict and I have remained in conflict, torn between the old world and the new for most of my life.

But back then I thought that I really had nothing to worry about because I was marrying the cowboy from Arizona and leaving the East for the West and an entirely new life. Part of me believed what I'd been taught by both experience and the nuns: that men should be obeyed, and that as a woman it was my goal in life to do everything possible to support my man, to trust his decisions, and to make a successful marriage—to love, to honor, and to obey, just as I would vow in the wedding ceremony; but another part of me knew that I had my own opinions, which might not always agree with my husband's, and that I too was important. I even wrote to Bill in a letter that I've saved all these years, "Remember, it's the hand that rocks the cradle that rules the world." I saw my power manifest in motherhood. Mary, the mother of God, was my model, and I strove to be unpretentious, simple, contented. I tried to rid myself of sophistication, superficiality, covetousness, unreasonable ambition, complexity, and duplicity, which I see now was nothing less than trying to be a saint on earth.

My conflict between being an old-fashioned Sicilian girl and a modern American girl arose almost immediately after our big family meeting. My brother, who was only a year older than I was, was essentially appointed the head of my immediate family. I was supposed to believe he knew better about all things because he was a boy. This I knew was proper and as it should be, but emotionally I resented anyone's trying to take my father's place, and intellectually I knew that my brother was no smarter than I was, and in my way I rebelled, which was interpreted as acting American.

It was the fall. I was writing Bill every day and he was writing me once or twice a week. This hurt my feelings and at the same time was understandable: He was in college and had important work to do, unlike me, who was idle, spending my days waiting for the mail and pining for him. After we'd moved into our new house, I'd helped my mother choose furnishings and generally set up the house, but now there was nothing left to do, and I saw no reason to stay home like a good Sicilian girl. Being very serious, pious, and idealistic, I believed wholeheartedly that idleness was the route to evil— and I suppose I still do.

So, one brisk fall day, without consulting my mother or my brother and knowing in my heart I would have the support of the nuns, I took my high school transcripts in hand, rode the subway to Finch College on the Upper East Side in Manhattan, and talked to the president, who declared that I was obviously a very bright and intelligent girl who absolutely should not waste her life and definitely should get an education—at his college. It would cost one thousand dollars for a year's tuition. I thought, sure, why wouldn't he say these things to me. Who couldn't use one thousand dollars. But then he said that if I had trouble raising the tuition, he was sure some sort of scholarship could be arranged.

I was flattered, and determined that I would go to college at least until I married, for three reasons: One was that I had a secret fantasy that I'd be the first girl in my family to graduate from college; the second was that I'd been taught by the nuns and believed that, given an emergency—if my husband were sick or had financial troubles—I should be prepared to work and earn money one day; and the third was that I believed going to college would make me a better wife. I would take liberal-arts courses and be able to hold my own in conversations I was sure to have with Bill and his college-educated friends in the future. I would take dress design and learn to sew all my own clothes; I would take home economics and learn the mechanics of cooking and the chemistry of a balanced diet.

After my meeting with the president I went directly to my brother's office—who at age nineteen had been thrust into running my father's business. Actually, my brother was a hard-working figurehead taking advice and orders from my uncle, who was calling all the shots. When I told him my plans, he went through the roof. He saw no reason why, especially if I was getting married, I would want to waste so much money in such a foolhardy way. Besides, it was improper for me to ride the subway and sit next to strangers every day. In short, he forbade it. I walked out of his office probably more angry than he was, but knowing better than to show it, and went directly to my mother, who voiced the same objections but was softhearted and always eager to do anything that might make me happier since my father had died. So, with much argument and tears on my part, they gave me the money and I was allowed to go to college.

When I wrote to Bill about my decision and the arguments with my family, he said he thought it best not to give his opinion. I interpreted this as approval but a reluctance to show disrespect to my mother and my brother by voicing it. Now that I look back on it, I probably interpreted much of what Bill said and did in those days in a rosy light because I wanted to believe that he was the perfect man.

CHAPTER 4

As it turned out I quit college after the first se-
mester anyway because I was much too busy with
the preparations for my wedding to have the time
or the interest to study. I've always been very concerned with making things look beautiful. Now I
threw myself wholeheartedly into realizing my vision of the most beautiful dress I could imagine. I
dragged my Aunt Vee, who had garment-industry
connections all over Manhattan, to look for the
right organdy and then for a person who could
hand-embroider my dress. I would hear nothing of
lace because it came off a bolt. I designed the dress
and cut the pattern out of muslin, which I pinned
to a form. The skirt was cut in several full circles.
Garden flowers with petals and pearls were hand-
embroidered on the bottom of the skirt and on the
bodice, which had a boat neckline and puff sleeves.
Daisies, my favorite flower, were embroidered on
the skirts of the dresses of my seven bridesmaids,
which I also designed. Bill's sister was my maid
of honor, and the other bridesmaids were cousins
from both families and children of our parents'
compares. One of these children's mothers had
called and pleaded for her daughter, whom I didn't

know, to be invited to be a bridesmaid, which was okay with me. I figured that if she wanted to that much and her parents respected mine so much, who was I to say no, although I must admit it puzzled me a little.

One day early on when my mother and I were beginning to plan my trousseau, we opened up a big trunk in which there were a few pieces from my mother's trousseau, and embroidered and hand-sewn sheets and nightgowns from her mother's trousseau, which my grandmother, whom I'd never known, had spent all her girlhood days working on. They were old, delicate, and breathtakingly beautiful in their simplicity. It filled me with warmth to think of the women in my family making the same sort of preparations for generations and generations. Then we found all the little sentimental love things my father had sent my mother before they were married: a flower from a bouquet that Papa sent Mama when she graduated from the eighth grade (that was 1929—she was fourteen, he was twenty-four); in 1930 an Easter card to "Sweetheart" signed "Tuo Turiddu"; a postcard from California that my mother said got her in trouble, which said, "Wish you were here" in English.

My parents were married in 1934. She was nineteen and he was twenty-nine. Like me with Bill, my mother had been in love with my father since she was a child. He'd shown up from Italy (except for the short stay in Canada and in Buffalo) at her uncle Joe Magliocco's house, where my mother was living because her parents had died when she was four. Since my father came from the same town, where the Profaci family were friends and allies with the Maglioccos, my great-uncle invited my father and his brother Joe Profaci to dinner every Wednesday and Sunday. They were also invited to bring their laundry, which my mother, at the age of eight, began to do. She told me how she'd been late for school one day and proudly told her teacher it was because she'd been ironing the shirts of Salvadore Profaci.

When Mama married Papa at nineteen, her aunt Fifi Magliocco, who had lived in the same house, had already married my father's brother Joe Profaci, and my father, without consulting my mother, had already bought my mother her house on Fourteenth Avenue and Eighty-third Street in Bensonhurst, Brooklyn, and furnished it with a houseful of furniture he'd bought at an estate sale. Beautifully carved antique mahogany pieces. My mother thought it not at all unusual that she had had no say in the choosing either of her house or of its furnishings, and so when I learned that Bill had chosen the house in Flagstaff where we would live after we married and where he'd continue his studies at Northern Arizona University, I didn't feel it was unusual either. But I had to admit to myself that I was a little disappointed because I had so looked forward to decorating my own home since I would be the one spending most of my time in it. Homes were and would continue to be very important to me. With my perfect husband, my perfect home would be the center of my perfect family. I consoled myself by being certain that my chance would come.

My father had also bought some huge paintings. One was a very beautiful and sumptuously dressed lady whom I dubbed the Contessa Viamonte and whom I spent many afternoons pretending to be. Now, with my wedding imminent, lots of money being thrown around, and practically my every whim indulged, I felt that I might have actually grown up to be the contessa. I fancied I was like Grace Kelly, who was also being married that year. My aunt Vee and I scoured New York shopping for my trousseau. Because it would be August and hot in Europe I decided on fine cottons. The dresses I chose were sewn as beautifully on the inside as on the outside, with perfect craftsmanship, which I knew something about. This was very important to me because I was a perfectionist. This makes me sound spoiled, and when I look back on it, I think perhaps I was, but in this I was encouraged by everyone around me.

I was very happy and very excited, but there had been a few hitches. The wedding arrangements had been taken over by—as my mother put it—"The Men," meaning Bill, his father, and my uncle, which in a way we didn't mind so much because the arrangements had become too mammoth and complicated for us to handle as the guest list steadily grew to three thousand. The only demand I made was that my reception not be held at the Commodore in New York, because that's where my two Profaci girl cousins got married, and mine wasn't going to be just another Profaci wedding.

Bill and I settled on the Sheraton Astor Hotel in Manhattan because it had the only ballroom large enough to accommodate all the guests. I have no idea what kind of deal was struck with the Sheraton Astor, the food preparers, the photographers, the filmmakers, the florists, the company from which we hired the dozen limousines—what favors were exchanged, what calling due on favors owed transpired. I do know that Peerless donated the liquor, and that the Sheraton Astor, which probably made the majority of its money from the liquor at such affairs, had nothing to say about it. Thousands of daisies would be flown directly from California to fill baskets that would be placed on every table. Tony Bennett would sing, as well as the Four Lads, and we would dance to Chic Cambria's orchestra.

This was all wonderful, of course, but it bothered me that I was seeing less and less of Bill, who was busy with all the details and running around doing whatever it was he did for and with his father. I would find out later that this wedding list was not only long but extremely complex and labor-intensive. The seating arrangements alone called for tremendous tact and diplomacy, since not only would there be judges and senators, but representatives of the twenty-four Families of their world, and some of these men still carried grudges and animosities from the old country. There was a certain hierarchy that had to be acknowledged, with the most important men placed closest to the dais so that new animosities and jealousies wouldn't arise. I would also find out years later from a book I read that this guest list had to be written in code so that the guests would remain a secret, because the FBI or whoever else was interested could have had a field day noting connections among people that nobody in my husband's world wanted made.

Just as Bill became increasingly distracted and busy and not there for me, my mother was getting more and more annoyed with him. She felt that the men were taking over, a state of affairs she was certainly used to, but which had been easier to take when it had been her husband and not her brother-in-law and Mr. Bonanno. The last straw came when Bill approached her and suggested that she should ask the priest to take a neon sign away from the front of St. Bernadette's before our wedding. The church was having a festival for the Feast of the Assumption, and there was a red neon sign that said THE ASSUMPTION in front of the church. My mother went to mass there several times a week, she was fond of the priest, and my father had donated a beautiful stained-glass window. She felt protective of the church and thought it was not her place to ask the priest to do any such thing. It would shame both the priest and herself. She thought it was a foolish request. She never told Bill this. She simply ignored him and the sign remained intact.

So, very close to the wedding, there was a little bit of discord, but much, much worse was that I had gotten my first inkling that everything might not be as I'd believed, that perhaps Bill was not the man I'd thought he was, and that I could very possibly be making a serious mistake. My misgivings arose after we took a ride in the moonlight and sat on a bench on Shore Road watching the lights twinkle on the water. (We now were allowed out alone.) It was a beautiful evening and I was very happy to cuddle up next to Bill, smell his familiar after-shave, and feel the weight of his arm on my shoulder. I felt very close to him and I told him how I thought of my father often, even more now that our wedding was near. I told Bill about how I'd wanted to tell my father to pray but had never summoned the courage and that if he were not in heaven it might be my fault. I told him my worst fear was that my father might be in hell, roasting for all eternity.

"I don't believe in that," Bill said.

"What?" I said.

"I don't believe in eternal damnation."

I was not very good at arguing or debating, while Bill was excellent at it, having been a member of the debating team in college. I knew that if I challenged him, he would end up winning the argument even though I had God on my side and was sure Bill was wrong, so I restricted my conversation to a few important questions. "You do go to mass every Sunday, don't you?" I asked.

"No, I don't."

"And after we're married?"

"What?"

"You still won't go to mass?"

"I'd say that's a fair assumption."

"So, then, you think it's all right to sin?"

"Sometimes it's necessary. Things are not black and white. Good and bad. Right and wrong. There are times when what may appear wrong to one person is right to another, especially if that person lives by a philosophy that in some ways is in conflict with the church's laws as they are interpreted literally, as you interpret them. In certain cases, a person who sees things the way you do might think I have sinned, and I might think I have simply done what I had to do."

This was abstract. I wasn't sure exactly what he was talking about but I was horrified. I believed if something is not right, it's wrong. I remembered how Bill had told me early on in our engagement that he was already wedded to something else, a particular philosophy of life, and that if during our marriage he had to choose between keeping the commitment and vow of that life-style and the commitment and vows of this marriage, he was serving notice now he would have to choose the first. I had asked him what he meant by this and he'd simply said, "I do what I have to do."

My husband says that his first commitment was to a tradition from the land of our fathers, a tradition born from the fragments of a burnt land. Every kind of invader had been lured to this jewel of an island strategically located along the most important trade route in the Mediterranean Sea. The Phoenicians took it, followed by the Greeks, Arabs, Normans, Spanish, and Bourbons. He explained that this tradition simply united the idea of beauty with the awareness of being a man, the sureness of soul. His foundation was faith in a Creator and the natural laws of life.

I was utterly confused.

It was a week before the wedding. Maybe I should pull out, postpone it, do something, but what? I believed what I loved, I loved out of goodness, and what I loved in Bill was what was good; and now I was forced to see that the man I was about to marry was not all good.

I think that when the nuns taught us what to expect in marriage, they forgot to include the husband.

The next morning I woke up with my whole body itching. My arms were covered with great red welts. I pulled the sheet off and lifted up my nightgown. They were all over my stomach too, only redder and larger. I ran into the bathroom and stared at the mirror in horror. My eyes were practically puffed shut. My first reaction was to giggle. This simply could not be. I couldn't possibly appear in front of three thousand people in my extraordinarily beautiful fairy-princess gown and have my face be one big angry blotch.

In a few seconds the laughter turned to tears and I wondered why God had seen fit to make my body break out like this. Maybe it was his way of telling me I shouldn't marry. But how in the world could I possibly get out of it?

Monsignor Rossi, a friend of the Bonannos whom they'd flown in from Arizona to marry us, was staying at the neighborhood rectory and had been coming by our house every day during the week before the wedding to eat his meals and simply to visit. I decided that that afternoon I would ask him to talk to me.

As religious as I was, I had never had a close relationship with a priest, and, in fact, other than confession, I couldn't think of a time when I'd actually talked to one. I was nervous as I sat in a chair on the porch next to Monsignor Rossi. I offered him a glass of lemonade by way of stalling, but he declined. I covered a welt on my hand with my other hand and said, "I'm having misgivings, Monsignor."

"Oh?" he said.

"I don't think Bill loves God the way I do."

"Oh, dear, dear, dear," he murmured. "I think maybe you just have a little of what we call the premarital jitters. It's natural."

"Father, I think I should postpone the wedding."

"Nonsense," he said a little too loudly. "You're overreacting. All young brides overreact. Remember, the family you're marrying is a fine family and Bill is a good young man. I've known him for years. He will make you a good husband. I think you know that. You've just been nervous with all the preparations and the pressure of such a big day. All you need's a good night's sleep. Now, how about that lemonade?"

Maybe he was right, because when I awoke the next morning, miraculously my welts were gone.

My wedding day was sweltering, 90 degrees and humid, but by now I was past feeling hot, I was past nervousness, I was well past corporeal considerations. I was a gorgeous showpiece and I played the role as though I were born to it. I beamed at the top of the aisle. I saw my handsome groom, tall and dark, waiting for me at the altar with a smile on his face, and I felt that any doubts, any troubles, any worries I'd had were foolish. Because this day was simply meant to be.

A movie camera recorded the event, and two photographers documented every moment and took carefully posed shots. And in these photographs and in the film, it looked as though everything had been rehearsed and staged because it all appeared so perfect, truly worthy of a movie, or, as some have said, like royalty—but, admittedly, of another world, one not usually associated with kings and queens, and princes and princesses.

After a filet mignon dinner, the guests came up one by one to wish us luck and to drop envelopes into a large satin pouch, which Bill's uncle Frank Labruzzo kept emptying to make room for more. The money we received filled a suitcase and totaled more than $100,000, which in 1956 was no small amount. My cheeks were red and raw from the kisses of so many men with heavy beards, my hand swollen from handshaking. My father-in-law was only fifty at the time and reigned over the whole event, debonair and gracious, dancing with the women, nodding to the men who were there more out of respect for him than for the bride and the groom, since I must have known no more than a hundred guests. I had heard that my uncle, in an attempt to match Mr. Bonanno guest for guest, had even invited the guy who sold him his Cadillacs.

My husband often left me to stand with his father. It warmed my heart to see them side by side, because I admired my father-in-law so much. But at various times during my engagement I'd resented this same closeness. It seemed as though Bill had been at his father's beck and call. But these thoughts were far from my mind now.

If there were powerful people jockeying for advantage or attention from Mr. Bonanno, as I have since been told, I was not aware of it. All I knew was that everything couldn't have gone more smoothly or looked more beautiful and that this was the happiest day of my life.

Back in our room upstairs, I changed into a negligee every bit as beautiful as my wedding dress had been, but much, much more delicate. It was made of fine white lace and was very sheer. Bill warned me when we began what I'd been waiting to do for years that making love would hurt, and it did, very much. I was surprised that I bled and a little disgusted and embarrassed at the stain on the sheets. Bill said, "Didn't your mother tell you?"

"I didn't know," I said.

"Didn't your mother tell you?" he repeated like he could not believe it.

My husband would continue to be surprised, really for the rest of his life, at the things my parents never told me.

We went to Paris and to Rome because I wanted to see Pope Pius XII, and then to Capri before ending our trip in Sicily. We bought beautiful furniture, small statues, and demitasse cups, which we shipped home with no regard for expense. Each hotel room we stayed in was filled with flowers and fruit and champagne. I was very naïve and had no idea of the arranging and the expense this had taken. If I had thought at all about it, I'm sure it was simply, *So this is what it's like when you travel in Europe.* I had never possessed any money of my own; it was always necessary to ask my mother or my father for money, then my brother, and now I would ask my husband. I'm sure we spent thousands and thousands of dollars on that trip, and I never had a dime in my own pocket, or thought it the least bit strange. I had no idea what a diamond ring cost, or a meal in a good restaurant.

Perhaps the first inkling Bill had of the frugalness I'd inherited from my father was in Capri. Bill found a beautiful gold watch from Persia that was encrusted with turquoise and diamonds. It was so beautiful it was breathtaking, but I said, "Bill, I already have a watch."

"What difference does that make?" he said.

"What would I do with two?"

He simply shook his head and gave up. For a few hours afterward he was quiet and seemed even sad. I did feel bad, but comforted myself with the thought of all the money I'd saved us, and before we left Capri I packed a starfish in my luggage. I had no idea it was a living thing and by the time we got home it stunk to high heaven.

The first hint I had of the world I would live in now was in Mondello, a beach outside Palermo. I awoke late one morning, about nine o'clock. After Bill and I bathed and dressed, he opened the door to our room to allow me to leave it first and I saw a man sitting next to our door with a gun in his belt. I gasped audibly.

"What?" Bill said.

"He has a gun," I whispered, though I didn't need to because the man probably didn't understand English.

"You mean to tell me this is the first time you noticed him? He's been with us since we landed in Sicily."

"Why?"

"Oh, you know Sicilians. We are all so suspicious you never can tell when there's going to be trouble. It's just for our protection. Don't worry about it."

I took Bill's advice and didn't worry about it, but thought that it was no wonder that I hadn't noticed him when we arrived in Palermo because there'd been such a big to-do. As soon as the plane landed, the stewardess called, "Will Mr. and Mrs. Bonanno please come forward and deplane first?" As we walked down the stairs a crowd erupted into cheers. A little girl handed me a bouquet of flowers, a woman kissed, then hugged me, while the men crowded around Bill, shaking his hand, hugging him, patting him on the back. They were relatives or friends of the Bonanno family, and I was impressed with the power and respect his family possessed even in Sicily.

In Castellammare del Golfo, the hometown of

the Bonannos, where we went after Mondello, we were greeted by a parade. A little band marched and girls held flowers as everyone followed Bill and me down the main street of town to a café where there was a big celebration with wine and food and dancing to honor the Bonannos. I wanted to go to Villabate, where my parents were from, but my husband said that it wasn't wise, that he'd been warned by my uncle to keep away. I didn't understand and didn't ask my husband more, and since I was accustomed to not asking questions, that was the end of the discussion.

When we returned to New York, we stopped over for only one night before we took the plane out west to Flagstaff, Arizona, and I began my new life as Mrs. Salvatore Bonanno.

CHAPTER 5

MARRIAGE was idyllic—at first. As soon as we arrived in Flagstaff, Bill and I both enrolled at Northern Arizona University, where I took drawing, art history, and literature classes. I sketched from real-life models in my drawing class and spent afternoons sitting on a rock or a log, painting the distant pine-covered mountains. When Bill had told me we'd be moving to Flagstaff, Arizona, I'd pictured it to be in the middle of a flat, sandy desert. I thought it would be as warm as summer all the time and had given my winter clothes to my little sister and younger cousins. But Flagstaff was high in the mountains, where snow could be seen in the distance, and the clear dry air invigorated me. Bill bought me a new winter coat and warm woolen sweaters. He also bought me my first pair of pants, which I was very modest about and would only wear when we went off on weekends, driving in our new Jeep up steep hills and into Oak Creek Canyon near Sedona, where buttes jutted into the air, a shocking red against deep blue skies. Bill told me, the city girl, stories about the different Indian tribes that lived on the land; how coyotes looked like dogs; how rattlers wouldn't attack unless attacked and that they loved warm places; how you had to shake your shoes out before you put them on because of centipedes; and how if you put an empty can over a scorpion it would kill itself. Bill was a good and patient teacher, and I admired his pioneer spirit. He was always ready to drive head-on into a crater or to ride a donkey down the Grand Canyon. I was proud of my cowboy husband.

He had deposited twenty thousand dollars in cash, which I assume was from our wedding, into the local bank and became instantly well-known. The bank manager began to stop by our house; all kinds of people approached Bill with ideas for investments. He joined the Kiwanis Club and we had great picnics at Lake Mary. He bought a share in a radio station and had his own music show at six-thirty each morning. We weren't there a month before everybody in town knew him, including every kid in our neighborhood. On Saturday mornings he'd invite the kids on our road in to watch Mickey Mouse movies. I'd make them popcorn and stay in the background as the kids yelped and jock-eyed for Bill's attention and I dreamed about having our own children. Bill, I knew, would make a wonderful father.

My husband, I came to realize, was a very social person. He thought nothing of saying to his professor and his class of ten or twelve, "Hey, why don't you come on home with me for dinner?" This is when I first developed my talent for making a meal appear in no time flat, which was one of the things about me Bill was most proud of. I made my dinners the Sicilian way, with a pasta dish followed by an entrée of meat and vegetables. Salads came last. Most of the people Bill invited over had never had pastas like I made and were very complimentary. But in those days, having studied nutrition and cooking at Finch College, I also liked "cooking American," which meant white sauces and popovers, soufflés and casseroles.

Our guests were kind and friendly, always remarking on how nice I'd made our home, which Bill had rented furnished and I had rearranged and added to with some wedding gifts and purchases from Europe. But I could not converse easily, had no opinions about foreign affairs, and little knowledge of anything really. I was afraid Bill's friends knew this about me, and I felt inferior. Besides, they were so strange. They were not Italian for one thing, and most of the women had DATED before they married, some of them SMOKED, and they thought it was perfectly natural to wear PANTS when they came to visit. When I told Bill how I felt ill at ease around these people, he got annoyed with me and accused me of being narrow-minded and closed. I knew this to be true, but I couldn't help myself.

I'd wanted to leave Brooklyn, but now I felt as if I were in a foreign country, homesick and strange at times. But there were many things I cherished about my new life. I loved ironing a shirt for Bill every morning and making sure he had balanced meals, I loved the vistas outside my windows, and I was learning to enjoy sex, which was a pleasure we experienced often in the middle of an afternoon, at the spur of the moment, and not always on a bed.

Bill did go away some weekends, saying that he had business to attend to or something to do for his father. I had to respect his following his father's wishes, because in our world a son would not think of refusing his father anything. But it did seem to me that his father made an awful lot of demands, and it worried me that Bill could just up and leave his studies for days without so much as a complaint, and that he could so easily leave his new wife as well. I'd imagined that once we were married we'd be inseparable, that we'd do everything together, and that he'd much rather be alone with me than have other people constantly visiting. One of the ironies of my life was that I never slept alone until I got married.

Then one weekend it came to a head and I got a glimpse of a side of my husband I didn't know existed. It was a Friday night. Bill was obviously preparing to leave. He'd taken a shower and shaved and had pulled his little valise down from the top of the closet. I said, "Bill, I don't want you to go."

He ignored me.

"I hate being left here alone. Can't you take me?"

"Stop whining. I'm sick of it. If I wanted to take you I'd take you."

"You never think about me. What I want."

Before I could see what was coming, he slapped me across the face.

I looked at him, stunned, my cheek smarting and tears brimming in my eyes.

"So, now you'll shut up. Huh?" he said as he walked out the door.

I felt horrible, humiliated, even though for a Sicilian woman of my generation, being hit by your husband was not unusual. We hit our pets to train them, we hit our children to make them behave, and men hit their wives for the same reason. But I'd never dreamed I could make Bill so angry he'd want to strike me. I was sure that I'd provoked him by being such a baby and that I'd deserved his anger. I felt bad for him because I knew he must be feeling horrible too, full of regret for what he'd done. I wished he loved me more so he would want to be alone with me as much as I wanted to be alone with him.

When he returned I tried extra hard. I made special desserts, and made an effort to be more lighthearted and to talk more when people were over. But when he left again the next weekend, I was mad. I decided that maybe I was being foolish. Maybe Bill would appreciate me more if I acted more brave and independent, more American. I packed a bag, withdrew money from the bank, and made reservations. I got on the plane for Phoenix, nervous as a cat. Not only because I was blatantly disobeying my husband, but because I'd never been on a plane alone before. Nor had I ever taken money from the bank. As soon as I got my room, I called Jackie, an English girl who dated one of Bill's friends, and asked her to meet me at a bar

Bill and I had been to. I was nervous but also flushed with excitement as I sat alone at a bar for the first time in my life. I ordered a highball and I noticed some men looking at me. I thought that maybe I should wait for Jackie outside, but then she walked through the door.

I didn't know Jackie very well, and in any case would never have thought it proper to tell tales about my marriage, so I simply said I was in town for the weekend without Bill. We chatted a bit about people we knew and she mentioned that Bill had been spending a lot of time in Phoenix lately, a fact I'd known nothing about. I had finished about half of my second drink when my husband walked through the door with his friend Tony. He smiled graciously and acted as though it were the most natural thing in the world to walk into a bar in Phoenix and find me sitting at it. "Well, well, if it isn't my beautiful wife," he said, smiling.

Tony kissed me on the cheek and struck up a conversation with Jackie, while Bill pulled up a stool and sat down. "So," he said, "taking a little vacation?"

"Umm, hmm," I said. "I came here by myself. I sat here alone, drinking. Jackie just got here a few minutes ago." I was hoping to make him jealous so he wouldn't take for granted that his little wife was always home waiting for him while he was off drinking at bars or doing whatever else he did.

"Did you smoke a cigarette too?" he said.

"No."

"And you got yourself a room at the Crescent?"

"How did you know?"

"Did you think you could do anything I wouldn't know about?"

I shrugged. The truth was I had no idea he would find me, and so soon, and I couldn't imagine how he'd managed it.

He took my arm and said, "What do you say we pay a visit to your room?"

There had been the possibility that he'd blow up at me, tell me to go home, even hit me again to teach me a lesson. Or worse, he'd just ignore me and go off and do what he'd planned to do along. So I was happy and relieved that the evening was about to take a turn toward the romantic.

But as soon as we stepped into the hotel room it was as though he became another person. Gone was the smile and any sign of affection as he began to strip off my clothes. When I stood there nude, he grabbed my pocketbook, shook its contents onto the bed, took the money, the keys to our house, and the bag I'd packed, and went to the door, where he turned and said, "Now you'll stay put."

I suppose this punishment made sense to my husband. I had acted free, so he would imprison me, which would make me think twice the next time I tried to run away. I understood the logic but I still cried all night, terrified that he might leave me in that room for days. Aware that I had been a bad girl and now was being punished—and feeling that I deserved it, especially since I'd defied my upbringing by my willful act of rebelliousness—I was relieved and very sorry when he returned the next afternoon and handed me my clothes. Neither of us said another word about it.

The next time Bill went away, he brought me a miniature dog to keep me company, which I appreciated even though I had no great fondness for animals.

And so, aside from the fight and my flight to Phoenix, our life was relatively tranquil for more than a year. I could picture myself living in this town forever, the wife of a well-respected lawyer who might even enter politics. The only wrinkle in my happiness was the fact that I had not yet conceived, which was more than a little upsetting because my main priority in life was to become a mother.

Then the Apalachin meeting of the Families happened and my world tumbled around me.

Bill had gone off for the weekend again, this time to hunt in Utah with some Tucson friends. I'd cooked myself some *minesta*, which is a soup with escarole in it, and turned the radio on to ward off the silence. I settled into the big chair next to the fire and picked up my art-history book to begin reading my assignment when the news came on and I heard the names Joseph Bonanno, Joseph Profaci, and Joseph Magliocco: my father-in-law and my two uncles. There had been a meeting of a reported sixty members of what the newscaster called organized crime in Apalachin, a town in upstate New York, at the home of Joseph Barbara, another familiar name. Could it really be that my family— my uncle, maybe my father, my father-in-law, even my husband—had been involved in this nefarious world? Suddenly I was sweating. In an instant I knew it was true. And in another instant, perhaps thanks to an unconscious conditioning I'd been subject to since the day I was born, I was trying not to think about it. But where was my husband? Had he been there too? Was he under arrest this very moment? I wished he would come home. Call me. Something.

The next morning I answered the phone and it was his father. I said, "Dad, hello. I've been so worried. What happened?"

He exploded, "Don't you know better by now? You don't ask questions on the phone. What is the matter with you?"

He'd never yelled at me before, but I'd heard him rage at Bill, so I wasn't as surprised as I was contrite. He was right. I was a fool. There was something the matter with me. I wasn't like other people. I was not like Bill's mother and my mother and the women of that generation, nor was I like the American Flagstaff women. I was distraught. I hated invoking my father-in-law's anger, but at least now I knew that my husband hadn't been in Apalachin, because if he had been there his father wouldn't be looking for him. Or maybe his father hadn't really been there either and was just calling his son to find out if anyone had contacted him. I wished Bill would hurry home, set my mind at ease, tell me it was nothing. But when he finally did arrive, he had heard nothing about the raid. I showed him the papers. He grew grim and silent, then threw them in the fire. After he talked to his father he said he was going out of town again. I didn't ask where or what for.

"When I'm gone," he said, "don't pay attention to anything you see in the papers. Anybody asks you questions, you don't know anything. Just tell them I'm away on business. You understand me?"

I nodded. I hoped he was simply being a good son and had no real interest in that other world beyond that. There had been many times when his father would call and almost instantly Bill would go running. His father had legitimate businesses—a cheese factory, a cotton farm, real estate holdings. I prayed that Bill had been helping his father with these and nothing else. But in my heart I knew that by wishing for this I was acting the fool.

"And for Christ's sake," he said as he was ready to leave, "watch what you say on the phone. The FBI are going to be listening now, do you understand?"

I nodded my head.

"When I call you, don't say my name, don't say anything, just listen."

"Why?" I ventured.

"I told you to listen to me. When I say *listen* it means don't speak. Don't ask questions. Jesus Christ, didn't your father teach you anything?"

He walked into the bedroom and called back, "Don't just sit there. Pack me enough for a week. I can have it laundered if I have to stay longer." When he left he peeled two hundred dollars from the wad of bills in his pocket and put it on the dresser.

Soon after that we left Flagstaff for good and moved in with Bill's parents in Tucson, where I learned some things.

The media was outside the house, knocking on the door, calling on the phone; the FBI was doing the same thing. My husband and his father were home much of the time, but my mother-in-law and I were never to let anyone know. So, when an FBI agent or a reporter called on the phone or knocked on the door and asked, "Is your husband or your father-in-law home?" it was not just a matter of saying no, because they were never satisfied with that answer. There always followed more questions, and those were the ones that got me into trouble, because I can't lie or make up stories for the life of me. When the FBI man or the reporter would say, "When did you see him last?" or "When do you expect him back?" or "Did he say when he'd be home?" I would always give the wrong answer. My mother-in-law, Fay, was better at this. She would defend her men no matter what. She was scared and angry and bold, but never timid. I wished I were more like her.

Then there was the matter of just plain answering the phone that will plague me for the rest of my life. I was supposed to try to get information from the caller without giving any information back. My husband yelled at me. My father-in-law frowned at me. My mother-in-law protected me. And I still couldn't do it right.

There was a lot of tension in the house and many meetings between men, so my mother-in-law and I tried to stay scarce. I took her shopping and visiting. I learned how to cook the way Bill liked by watching her. She was a good cook but favored simple food. She used fewer spices than the women of my family. I wondered if my aunts back in Brooklyn were under siege too. If my father had lived, would my mother be scared to answer the phone or go to the door? My mother couldn't lie either. I remembered that when I was a child there were times when my brothers and sisters and I were told not to answer the phone. I also remembered being sent to a neighbor's on an errand. When I got to the door a policeman answered it and pointed a gun in my face. I ran home crying. Could it be true what my husband was always implying? Had my father been involved in that world that the newspapers were calling the underworld? I decided not to think about it.

Then I asked Bill one afternoon when we'd be going back to Flagstaff so that he could complete law school, he said, "We're not."

"What do you mean?"

"Just what I said. My priorities have changed."

I began to face the fact that my husband was not a cowboy or a lawyer, or a politician, or even a businessman.

Bill spent less and less time at home, often leaving without saying where he was going or when he was returning, which he had done before. But now he showed no regret, only arrogance in his right to do as he pleased. He must have been under a great deal of pressure, but he never confided this to me. I know that he made many trips to New York to help his father with the Apalachin trial, and that he and his father had had tremendous real estate holdings in Arizona, but now, with the adverse publicity, the banks were calling notes due. I imagine Bill was hustling and trying to save as much of his and his father's interests as he possibly could, but I knew none of this at the time. All I knew was that my husband wasn't around.

I began to realize that as deluded as I'd been about my husband before we married, he was also deluded about me. He was only twenty-three years old and believed, like any good Sicilian boy, that he'd married because it had been time to take a wife, give her a house, a car, a couple of kids, and then go off and do whatever the hell he pleased, which could even include seeing other women, and that the good Sicilian girl he married would accept everything.

Bill had also thought that because I was the daughter of Salvatore Profaci I had been educated in the ways of his world, that I knew what it was all about. He'd thought that by marrying me he was marrying someone as savvy as his mother, a girl who would keep her mouth shut, not ask questions, and never complain, a girl he wouldn't have to break in. It was around this time, the time of our first entrenchment from the FBI and the media, that Bill began to say that when he married he'd thought he was getting one thing but got another. A lemon was the word I used.

Many things were different now. We could not have a savings or checking account, or credit cards. Everything had to be paid for in cash so there would be no record of spending. The Bonanno name had been all over the Tucson papers and editorial writers were asking that we be driven out. The town did not wish to be infiltrated with underworld characters from the East.

Within a few months Bill found us a house in Tucson, again without first consulting me, and this one I hated. It was out in no man's land, the last house on a road in the foothills. I heard coyotes every night and was so scared I went to sleep as soon as the sun set to avoid the darkness whenever Bill wasn't home, which was half the time. Practically every time he returned from being away he brought home another guard dog, first a Weimaraner, then a German shepherd, a poodle, and a Doberman, hoping they would make me less frightened, but I was as afraid of the dogs as I was of the darkness. But, I rationalized, where else would a cowboy live?

I was more lonely than ever, so Bill urged me to go out and make some friends. But even if there were people I could be comfortable around, I was so shy and withdrawn, I probably wouldn't have felt really at ease with them until I knew them for a couple of years. There were many nice women in Tucson, which was Bill's hometown, old friends of his family who were sympathetic to us and nonjudgmental about what they read in the papers, but I had nothing in common with the single women or the married ones, who were either working women, young mothers, or socialites. I was none of those things. Besides, I did not understand some of these Americans. If you visited they didn't put the coffee on right away and offer you something to eat. Most people weren't Italian or Catholic, and besides, some of the women Bill thought I should be friends with had been divorced. I couldn't imagine befriending a person who had committed such an irrevocable sin, and I was not accustomed to looking outside my home for fulfillment.

I joined a ceramics workshop at Bill's urging, where I made a Bonanno crest-of-arms ashtray, which I gave to my father-in-law. I began a couple of oil paintings and started to redo some furniture to keep myself busy, but I was growing increasingly depressed and disappointed in the way my marriage was going. I was sure that nine months after I married I'd have a baby. But it was going on two years and I still hadn't conceived. Everybody I knew got married and had babies. I went to doctors who said my uterus was tipped, which would make it difficult to conceive. I felt like damaged goods, like I wasn't an authentic she-woman. I became obsessed with the workings of my body and furious with Bill because he didn't seem involved enough.

I was on an emotional roller coaster. Every menstruation was followed by devastation, as month after month great expectations were followed by periods of mourning. I felt victimized by fate and was angry. Motherhood was the goal of my life. What if it were denied me? I knew that God had a plan and that I had no idea what that plan was, but still I could not take this. I just couldn't understand. Perhaps I was displacing all my disillusionments and disappointments with life onto my failure to get pregnant.

Bill had things to do in the world and I had nothing. If I had had a child to care for, I wouldn't have been so dependent and focused on Bill. I wouldn't have cared so much that he left me alone so often or that we never really talked. And perhaps if I hadn't been so needy he wouldn't have found it so necessary to run away from me.

Finally I went to see Dr. Lacock in Tucson on my mother-in-law's recommendation. He told me that only one of my tubes was partially opened and the other was completely blocked. When he injected oil in order to X-ray my tubes, miraculously the oil unblocked them. I soon conceived and thanked St. Gerard, the patron Saint of Mothers. It was as though my world turned around overnight. I was thrilled. Bill was thrilled. We called everybody. I made beautiful maternity dresses. We both enjoyed my new body. I had 36C breasts and felt sexy. We were both very happy, and marriage, again, was blissful.

The house we'd moved into was all pine paneling and had exposed beams in the interior, which I had no taste for, coming from New York as I did. It seemed like the house wasn't finished. When I started to prepare the nursery I thought it was too dark, so I had the panels painted white enamel and the beams red, yellow, blue, green, and purple, and had no idea what a sacrilege that was. I bought a crib and a changing table. Bill's sister gave me a lovely shower and the room was filled with stuffed animals, rattles, mobiles, and the drawers stuffed with diapers and Dr. Dentons.

Bill was home with some friends the night I began labor. They timed the minutes between contractions. I made them ham sandwiches and Bill handed out beers. It was all very festive and wonderful.

I never saw the baby. When I awoke from a shot the doctor had given me I asked the nurse what I had and she said my husband would be right in to talk to me. When he came in he told me that the baby wasn't strong enough to survive the birth. We named her Phillipa after Bill's mother, according to Sicilian tradition, and he and his sister buried her before I left the hospital.

Friends told Bill that it would be best to erase all traces of the baby to help me get over the loss. So when I arrived home, the baby's room was empty. I was inconsolable. Bill, in his desire to help me forget, had organized a dinner with friends at a restaurant. They'd just uncorked the wine when I fainted and Bill had to take me home. I hardly spoke for months. I slept constantly, and cried every morning and every night. Bill stayed home more than he had since we were first married. He arranged for a vacation to California. He brought me to nightclubs, where I stared off into the distance like a zombie. I didn't want fun and distraction, I wanted comforting and time to mourn my loss, but Bill, being the gregarious person that he was, thought that what I needed was a good time to cheer me up.

When I look back on the attention Bill paid me and his kindnesses, I feel grateful. He would have given me anything. If I'd asked that we go on a safari to Africa he probably would have taken me. I was uncommunicative, tearful, and mopey as soon as I opened my eyes in the morning, while Bill opened the curtains to let the sun in and tried to make jokes to put a cheerful face on things. But I would have none of it, and Bill never lost his temper. If I'd been in a better frame of mind I would have consoled myself with this evidence that my husband really did love me. During this time it never occurred to me that Bill had also lost a child.

We kept trying to make me pregnant, but I was afraid now that it would never happen again. God had given me a dead baby and it might have been a sign or a judgment.

Meanwhile, Bill opened a food warehouse where he put me to work in the office doing bookkeeping to help me keep busy and distracted. The office was large and beautiful with big stuffed chairs, a sofa, a hi-fi, and brand-new filing cabinets. I couldn't understand why he needed such a gorgeous office at a warehouse. I thought maybe there was something going on there that I had no knowledge of. I later learned this was the central office for various businesses of my husband's. They were R&B Enterprises, Inc., a real estate and investment company, an insurance agency, two fast-food restaurants, a real estate company, and, of course, a warehouse. And I still didn't know why he traveled so often and for such long periods of time. He would tell me many years later that the Profacis— the Family that shared my maiden name and was part of the other world I had so little knowledge of, or, really, curiosity about—were in trouble in New York, and that my uncle Joe Magliocco and two other men had been kidnapped in Florida. This was part of the headlined Gallo-Profaci wars. The Profaci family was in danger. But eventually, when he tried to get my cousins to help defend it, they were too involved in their own businesses and not very willing to risk their lives to save my uncle Joe. This infuriated my husband because even though he was of the first American-born generation, as were my cousins, Bill was the only one who seemed to feel a loyalty and commitment to a tradition that took action against wrongs and saw it as a point of honor to do so.

I knew nothing of all this at the time, and had I known, I probably would have sided with my cousins, believing that it was more important to take care of your immediate family than this larger family, where death, trouble with the law, or bankruptcy were often the prices that had to be paid. And because Bill was out of town so much, the warehouse was going down the tubes. I became more and more frightened. I felt that Bill, so often out of temper with me and so distracted when he was home, simply didn't like me. His life away from me was more important, and I was in his way.

One evening after Bill had been away again for several days, I awoke to hear him come into the house. I didn't bother to get up or turn on the light because it was very late and I'd been in the middle of a deep sleep. I was barely conscious. When I heard him come into the room and felt him place something on the bed. It was warm and it moved. I assumed it was another dog and rolled away to the edge of the bed, but then it made a distinct baby sound and I sat up. There, sitting on the bed looking at me, was a baby around a year and a half old.

"Whose is it?" I said.

"He's yours," he said.

"Aw, come on, Bill."

"He's yours. He's ours. Don't ask any questions. Just treat him as if you gave birth to him."

I stared at the baby in disbelief. Bill walked into the bathroom and I heard the shower go on. I looked closer at the baby. It was a boy and he was wearing a blue sleeper. One of his eyes had a droopy lid, and his hair was light brown and cut in a butch. I could see that his ears were dirty. He didn't cry or fidget or act at all frightened. He just sat there looking at me like this was the most natural thing in the world, to be sitting on a strange bed in a strange house staring at a strange lady. "What's your name?" I said, even though I should have known he was too young to talk much.

He smiled.

I held out my arms. He held out his arms.

And this is how my first child came to me. We named him Charles and called him Chuck. By the next day he was calling me Mommy and soon we were inseparable. When I put him down for a nap I would stare at him and wait for him to wake up. He ate everything and helped himself. He'd climb onto counters and open cabinets, using drawers as steps. He was forever letting the dogs in. I took him everywhere, and if he was tired he feel asleep on my arm.

Bill told me how he'd put out the word that he was looking for a baby and how someone had found a woman in Los Angeles who'd just moved from Virginia and had no money but wanted her son to have a good home. Bill said that when she gave him Chuck, he had only one shoe, the diaper he was wearing, and a T-shirt. Bill left Chuck with his friend in a hotel and went to a big department store to buy him clothes. The jeans he bought were about a foot too long and had to be rolled up several times. When Bill drove back to Arizona, Chuck stood on the seat between him and his friend, wide awake and uncomplaining the whole way. Then they brought him to Joy, his friend's wife, and asked her to give him a bath. After that he brought Chuck to me.

Bill took Chuck's bottle and blanket away the first day because no son of his was going to need a bottle and blanket. Then he had his cousin Frank dig a sand pit and bought Chuck some cars and trucks to play with.

I guess you could say Chuck did the trick, because it was right after Bill brought him home that I relaxed enough to get pregnant again.

I hoped now that we were a real family Bill would spend more time at home, but Bill continued to spend days and nights away and seemed more distant than ever, so I stepped up my campaign at self-improvement, determined that if I were only prettier and the house always spotless and the meals I cooked lavish and delicious, it would do the trick. I would entice my husband to stay home and find contentment. But there were times when I'd cook dinner and put it on the table only to watch him walk out the door without an explanation. One time, I'd had enough and began to throw food at him. He dodged a plate and walked out. Before he came back I'd cooled down enough to be ashamed of my behavior.

Bill was preparing to go out of town. My labor pains started at eight in the morning. Bill brought me to the doctor, who said I could expect to have the baby in a week, so Bill thought it would be safe for him to go. By eleven that night I was sure I was in labor and called my father-in-law to take me to the hospital. I knew that if anybody could get the word to Bill, it would be Joseph Bonanno. Bill was there when Joseph came into the world screaming his head off. He was a beautiful and healthy boy and I thought Bill would be thrilled, bring a bottle of champagne and pop it or something, at least give me a big kiss and a hug, but he seemed quiet, even subdued, as though his mind were elsewhere, or the birth had provoked some deep thinking. It never occurred to me that his mind went back to the time of our firstborn. Bill had seen both children at birth and was in awe of the miracle of this baby's perfection.

People from all over sent flowers. There were so many that they filled the room and then lined the hallway. According to Sicilian tradition, the first son is named after the paternal grandfather. And so I wrote Joseph Bonanno on my baby's birth certificate. I gave him the middle name of Gerard, after the saint I'd been praying to for five years. Later, at Joseph's baptism, Bill gave Joseph his godfather's name of Gregory, the name my son grew up to use, which would cause him no little difficulty when it came time to file official documents because the name Gerard is still on his birth certificate.

Joseph was a sickly baby who never developed the knack of sleeping through the night. By the time he was twenty-two months old he had developed asthma, which is usually linked to emotional stress, which God knows he probably caught from his mother. I was not your cool, calm, everything-is-right-with-the-world mommy, although I do think I was born with an instinct for mothering. It was not Joe or Chuck who was making my world turn upside down but the fact that when I came back from the hospital I'd found a lipstick stain on my husband's underwear, and also discovered that the bed had not been slept in, which only confirmed the suspicions I'd been having for years: My husband had another lover.

I confronted him and he flew into a rage. "I'm sick of your bitching, your moods! You're never happy! Now you're going to start imagining things. You wanted a baby. You got two babies. You're still not happy."

"What is she? A tall, busty blonde? An American? I bet she swears. You like that, don't you?"

He grabbed me and spun me around. I ended up with a bruise on my arm. After a while I gave up confronting him and questioning him because I got only denials and sometimes a slap. I was too ashamed to tell anyone this, but when I'd appeared in his sister's wedding with a bruise on my upper arm in plain sight, I think I secretly hoped someone would notice and ask me what happened. Nobody did. One time after he hit me I called my mother and asked her to send me money so that I could come home. She said, "This is between you and your husband. You solve your problems in your home."

"But he hit me."

"Well, what did you do? You must've done something to make him mad."

My mother believed, like most Sicilian women of her generation, that when a woman married she belonged to her husband, and if he hit you it was his right. I too had been schooled in this tradition, and so had my husband. Consequently, whenever I invoked his anger, I turned inward and wondered how I could have avoided it and why I was so stupid as not to know when to keep my mouth shut.

Still, I was unhappy. I had my two children and I wanted a real home with a father in it for them, so I decided to talk to Bill's father. I told him that I was unhappy because Bill was not being a good husband. Mr. Bonanno repeated an Italian saying, "Eat the *minesta* or throw yourself out the window."

Obviously, I'd better keep my troubles to myself.

By now the warehouse had failed, and Bill moved us to Phoenix, where he was the manager of a club called the Romulus. Practically the only time I saw my husband alone was when we were sleeping, because he always had someone with him. We were in yet another rented and furnished house, and I was getting sick of the moving around and the insecurity. I'd become a chronic complainer. I wanted my own house. I felt that he must have blown all our wedding money, and that he could have at least bought me a house with it. Bill seemed to have less and less money, and I had no money of my own. Whenever I went to the grocery store I had to ask Bill for cash. Bill's father's defense in the Apalachin trial had cost hundreds of thousands of dollars. Tax agents had begun to investigate Bill's income from the wholesale food warehouse and from real estate holdings, and he would soon be charged with income-tax evasion, the agents claiming he owed $160,000 in back taxes. Then Bill bounced a check for $1,930, and although he made restitution, he had to go to court, which elicited more publicity. Bill was placed on probation for three years.

The Romulus was not doing a very good business either, because police began to stop the customers as soon as they drove out of the parking lot and test them for alcohol consumption. It seemed that there was a concerted effort to harass my husband, and he was acting harassed. When he was home he was distracted and critical. Besides, I knew in my bones that Bill had a girlfriend but I could prove nothing.

Since it seemed to me my presence meant precious little to my husband, I decided to leave him— even though it wasn't freedom I wanted but to be loved and sheltered. As soon as I boarded the plane to New York, I regretted my impulsiveness, and when it landed due to mechanical difficulties, I was convinced Bill had made it happen and became hysterical. The next day I knew I'd have to make something come to a head, so the next time he appeared wearing a shirt I hadn't seen for months, I asked him who'd laundered it. He said it was the woman who lives across the road from his brother Joe. When he left that day, I loaded Joseph, who was now two, and Chuck, now four, into the car and drove to the house across from Bill's brother. There, in the driveway of a house practically identical to mine, was a green Falcon, exactly the same color and model as the one I was driving.

I very calmly got out of the car and knocked at the door. Erica, a German woman, answered. She was pregnant. She invited me in. There was the box of tissues on the kitchen counter where Bill likes to keep one. I glanced into a bedroom as we passed it and saw a picture of her and Bill on her night table. She asked me if I'd like to sit down, then excused herself to go to the bathroom. As Chuck was helping Joe off with his sweater, I ran into the bedroom and looked in the closet. Half of it was filled with Bill's clothing.

When she returned I said, "How long have you been intimate with my husband?"

"I think I'd better call him," she said and left the room.

When she returned again, I said, "Do you love my husband?"

"Yes, I do," she said.

"Is that his baby?" I said.

"Yes," she said. "I love him very much. Can I get you anything, tea or coffee?"

I began to foam at the mouth. This had never happened to me before and would never happen again. I felt as though my mouth were filled with cotton, but actually it was thick white foam and it was spilling out of the corners of my mouth.

Bill was there in a matter of minutes. He walked into the room and said, "Get in the car," which I did, then he drove me and the kids home while one of his friends drove my car back.

Neither of us said a word for hours. The children were in bed and I walked into the kitchen, where he was drinking a glass of Coke at the table. I said, "She probably thinks you're a big shot. She thinks you're great."

"Watch your mouth," he blew up. I was afraid to say another word because he could get dangerous. I decided that if he really loved her and wanted her, he should have her.

But in the days that followed, I was not so willing to give him up. I kept thinking, *What does she have that I don't?* I'd try to win him back, because I loved him and there was no one else to take care of me and the children, and because I was only twenty-five and could not imagine living the rest of my life without sex. I never considered having another man. For one thing it would be a sin, and for another, I didn't even know how to talk to a man who wasn't either a teacher, a priest, or a relative, and couldn't imagine one even touching me.

There was only one course of action for me and that was to try even harder. I was never seen with rollers in my hair or without makeup. I wore stockings every day. There was no dirty laundry or ever a dirty dish left in the sink. There was always fruit arranged decoratively on the table, food ready to be prepared at an instant's notice. After that incident, my husband made sure that he always came home for at least an hour every night and stayed out all night only if he was going out of town.

This hyperhousewifery was getting harder to maintain, however, because in a year I had Tore. When Bill saw him after I delivered, he sat on the bed, his elbows on his knees, his face in his hands, and wept. This was the first and last time I would ever see him cry. His tears were from happiness. Tore was a very unhappy and colicky infant, however. Like Joseph he never slept, and now I had two babies up every night. The only calm presence in the house was five-year-old Chuck, who was always on hand to help me by walking over to the pail to throw a dirty diaper in or by picking up the toys after Joseph or by just entertaining us by being a clown.

It was obvious to me by now that Erica and Bill were having a hard time. Bill was looking awful, his temper was shorter, and he was spending more time at home. Then one evening, when Tore was about two months old, Bill said, "I want you to do something for me. A favor. And if you do it, I'll be indebted to you. I'll owe you back and I'll make everything right again. I don't want you to ask any questions. Just believe this must be done. After it's done whatever has been going on with me and Erica will be over, although when I tell you what it is you have to do you will think the opposite. Just trust me. Believe what I tell you. And do what I say."

On the ride to Erica's he continued. "It's not a pretty sight; you don't know what's gone on, and I don't want you making up stories in your head about it. Just believe me when I tell you, what is had to be."

We did not go to Erica's house as I'd expected, but to another house where another woman answered the door. Bill guided me into a bedroom where Erica was lying in a bed. She was beaten up. Her eyes were swollen from crying. I began to tremble because I knew I was about to do what Bill had asked me, and I also knew it would haunt me for the rest of my life. I sat next to the bed and did not look in her eyes as I lied, "Bill and I are getting a divorce. He's in love with you and I'm letting him go."

Then I left.

I told a lie. My husband deceived me, pierced my self-esteem, and had broken the sacred vow of fidelity. This was against everything I believed, everything I strove for. The nuns always said: "Your purity and chastity will be appreciated by your husband. Life will reward your self-control, your goodness. You must give the man you marry an untarnished rosebud."

I have never been the same.

I couldn't sleep after that. Joseph's asthma got worse. Tore slept maybe for a total of eight hours each day. I tried to sleep when they did, but their sleeping times were so few and far between, and I was so upset and overwrought, I could not find the peace to release my mind, let go, and fall asleep.

So, one day, when I knew Bill was expected home in a few hours, Chuck was asleep for the night, and the babies would be asleep for a while, I took a sleeping pill. I hoped it would knock me out, then Bill would come home and have to take over. It didn't work, so I took a second and waited fifteen minutes. It didn't work, so I took a third and was out like a rock. When Bill came home he couldn't wake me, but I do remember in a cloudy way that he made me vomit then brought me to the hospital, where I have a vision of being surrounded by policemen. The next day was Mother's Day and Bill had me call my mother to tell her I was fine and to wish her a happy Mother's Day. But no one answered.

My "suicide attempt" had made the headlines. My mother read about it and didn't even finish her laundry before she caught the next flight to Arizona.

CHAPTER 6

THE newspapers called my pill-taking a suicide attempt. The stories they wrote were small, but above them was my picture. This was the first of many times my picture would appear in the paper, and I was appalled at how public my life had become. I felt that somehow it was a form of punishment for the lie I had told Erica. I was worried about the pain this would cause my mother, and distressed about the untruth of it all. If I had tried to commit suicide it would have meant I'd succumbed to despair, and I've always believed despair to be the greatest sin. No matter how bad I have felt, no matter how hard life has seemed, I have always held on to the belief that God would take care of me.

I kept holding on to the thought that God would take care of my children too, because when I asked Bill where they were and who was caring for them he refused to answer. This was the worst punishment of all. I was numb and exhausted as I lay in that hospital bed in a private room. There was a bouquet of daisies on a stand next to me, but I didn't know who'd sent them. I wept silently and prayed and waited until I could go home.

By the time I was released my mother had arrived and my children were safe and happy in her care. I was utterly relieved and grateful that my mother was with me. She took charge of my babies and tried to marshal them into the kitchen each morning before their cries could wake me. She scrubbed my floors and scoured the bathroom. She opened the windows to let in fresh air. I think what I mostly felt as I lay in bed all day and night was not anger at my husband but a longing to be snuggled against the warm bosom of my mother. To prolong this feeling of safety. So when my mother suggested I come home with her I felt a quickening in my heart, a hint of the vitality that comes with relief, and we both proceeded to ask Bill if it would be okay for me to leave with my mother.

The reason we gave for my going to Brooklyn was that my sister Annie was getting married in a couple of months. I was to be her maid of honor, and both she and my mother could use my help. This was true, but only partly. Both my mother and I, being Sicilian women, knew without talking about it that if we said I needed desperately to get away from Bill and my life, to catch my spiritual breath in an attempt to feel renewed, there would be no way in the world his pride could allow it. So, Bill agreed to let me return to Brooklyn, and I think he may have even known the real reason I was leaving but the important thing was not to voice it.

On the plane ride home, between trying to keep Chuck and Joe seated and the baby, Tore, quiet, I began to empty my heart to my mother. I told her that Bill had been having an affair for what I believed to be six years. I told her about the nights he never came home. I told her I'd given up arguing with him because of his rages. She patted my knee as I spoke, shook her head, and made comforting sounds.

"But I love him, Mama," I said. "After everything, I'd do anything to get him back."

"Shhh, shhh," she said.

Life at my mother's was like paradise. Both my sisters, Victoria, fifteen, and Annie, twenty-one, were at home; my brother Frank was in a seminary, but my older brother, Sal, was home too. Everyone helped care for and entertain the children, and my mother made three wonderful meals a day for all of us. I had forgotten what it was like to be encircled by my brother and sisters—the spontaneous laughter, the way it feels to be with people who know who you are deep inside and accept you for it, the way they help without asking, the warm feeling you get from being near people who love you. I felt as though I were slowly waking from a bad dream. At night after I'd put the children down, my sisters and I would sometimes sit on our beds like in the old days and gossip. They filled me in on my cousins, their marriages, and the personalities of their children. I began to fantasize about how wonderful it would be if I lived nearby. I could see all my cousins. We could raise our children together. There'd be big Sunday dinners like when I was a kid. If I could only get Bill to live back East, then I'd have my family around for help and support and wouldn't be so totally dependent on him for affection.

Since my cousins had married into the same world in which I'd found myself, I would do as my cousins had done: stick to my own kind. My sisters and mother would drop by. They'd baby-sit. Maybe there was a way for Bill and me to be happy.

Bill and I had spoken on the phone over the weeks, but our conversations were never about our troubles. Mostly he asked after the children and I told him how Chuck was as cheerful as ever, how Joseph's coughing was sporadic and nothing to worry about, and how Tore had slept up to six hours at night a couple of times. We never said "I love you" to each other.

I was numb, and I was worried. It's true that I'd reached a breaking point, that I'd retreated to my mother's. But I never once considered that I was leaving my husband, and the only time divorce came to my mind was when I wondered if he might want one from me. So when he called one night to say he was leaving Arizona to come and get me, I was relieved at the same time that I was beside myself with fear. I did not want to go back to that desert out there, ever. My family was at dinner, and when I returned from the phone to the table I said, "Bill's coming. I'm going to be so sad to leave."

"So don't go," Annie said. "Refuse."

"I can't," I said.

"Why not?" she said.

I couldn't answer. My mother didn't say "Annie" in a stern voice like she did so many times when Annie stepped out of line. Still, I doubted I'd ever have the courage to refuse.

When Bill arrived in Brooklyn, he went to his Aunt Rose's instead of to my mother's, then he sent his Aunt Rose and Aunt Marion to fetch me and the children to him. I remembered how unimportant Bill could make me feel, how just plain awful. Though we put calm and contented faces on for Bill's aunts, my mother and sisters and I were outraged that Bill didn't come for me himself. What they didn't know was that with my family around I found courage. (I would learn later that Bill hadn't been sure what to do himself. I was, after all, staying in the house with my brother, who was a Profaci, and there had not been a great deal of affection between the two men since my husband had decided that my brother did not act honorably during the Gallo-Profaci disturbance.)

After cake and coffee and idle chatter, Bill's aunts finally realized I wasn't budging, so Aunt Rose excused herself to make a phone call from the other room. I assumed she called Bill, who gave them permission to leave. They left almost immediately, and although they said nothing, I felt that they were shrugging their shoulders and shaking their heads at that loony Profaci girl their nephew married.

That night I lay in bed thinking about my marriage. These weeks with my family had thrown a different perspective on my thinking. My uncertainty came rushing back. I even flashed back to my thoughts and feelings those last few days before my marriage. I still wasn't sure if this was the right life for me. I remembered washing my hair at least every other day and setting it every day. I remembered brushing my hair until my scalp felt raw to give it a sheen that would make me prettier. I remembered racing to the bathroom before the babies or Bill awoke so I could wash the mascara from under my eyes before Bill got up and saw me. I twisted myself like a pretzel to please him. I pictured myself in the kitchen: I squeezed fresh orange juice, then Bill criticized me for the pits in it; I buttered his toast and he asked me where I bought the butter; I served him cereal and he asked me the date on the milk. I put on a skirt and he said it was too short or too long. I saw that no matter how hard I tried it wasn't good enough. I knew now he'd been comparing me to Erica.

I wondered if Bill would be happier with Erica. I obviously didn't know how to please him. Maybe I should have gone with his aunts. I wondered if I didn't go with them because I had to save face in front of my mother and sisters. In spite of my fear and anger, I missed Bill.

In the morning, at first, everyone was full of bravado and indignity, talking about what a nerve my husband had, not to come for me himself and make peace with his wife. But then, almost immediately, we started to worry. My mother had beautiful new furniture in her house for my sister's wedding. What if he came and made a scene? What if he brawled with my brother and wrecked the house?

As it turned out, our fears were justified. What

I'd been viewing as my being secure in my family's bosom my husband had been seeing as my being garrisoned off away from him by the Profaci family. He showed up the next afternoon in a fury.

I grabbed Joseph and ran out the back door, while Vickie and Annie hid in the bathroom with Tore. We couldn't find Chuck, who was playing in the pantry. As soon as Bill burst through the door without knocking, my mother flew at him like a banshee. She grabbed his coat and shook him with all her might, screaming in his face, "Get out of my house! Leave my daughter alone! If you hurt her again I'll kill you!"

Bill had never raised his voice to my mother, and he didn't now. Instead he focused his fury on my brother, who sat in a big chair in the living room watching. "Look at you, hiding behind your mother's skirts like a woman. Get the hell up and fight like a man." My brother, wisely, just sat there, his eyes locked on Bill's, not moving a muscle. He knew that if he lifted so much as a finger my husband might lose it.

Meanwhile, Chuck heard the commotion and came running from the pantry shrieking in delight, "Daddy, Daddy!" Bill tore away from my mother and scooped up his oldest son, then ran up the stairs looking in all the bedrooms and closets, and finally banging on the bathroom door. Vickie yelled, "Don't come in; I'm in the tub," and Bill left, vowing that he'd return the next day and warning that I'd better be there with his kids or else.

We were dazed. My mother sat down, the red-ness only now leaving her cheeks. She fanned her bosom. "I never heard of such a thing in my life. These people. They're so different."

I wished my brother would say something reassuring. He seemed deep in thought, actually very calm. I think he was thinking that we may have just escaped a domestic battle. I admired him for having kept his cool, although I knew my husband would think him a coward. Anger is the wind that blows out the mind, I always say. Sal stood up. "Come on," he said, "we're going to the shore."

Was he afraid Bill would come back and make more trouble? Was my brother going to call somebody up and start trouble himself? How had my brother felt allowing Bill to trample through his mother's house? Would this result in a Profaci-Bonanno incident that would be all my fault? I did not ask any of these questions and neither did anyone else. I wondered if my sisters and mother were wondering the same things.

We packed some clothes and piled into my brother's car, then drove to the New Jersey shore. When my brother parked in front of a two-story house on the ocean, we all climbed out, then took naps.

The next evening we got a call from my great-uncle Joe Magliocco. My uncle Joe Profaci had died the previous year, and Uncle Magliocco had become the head of our family. Uncle Magliocco was also my baptismal godfather. We hadn't told him anything about what was going on, but Bill obviously had decided to go the official route be-

cause my uncle knew everything and had somehow
tracked us down to tell us to get the hell back to
Brooklyn. He told my brother that he must be out
of his mind and that he'd better turn right around
and bring me back to Bill. I was Bill Bonanno's
wife first and Sal's sister second. My mother had
grown up in Uncle Magliocco's house and was not
as frightened of him as she'd been of Joe Profaci.
Besides, my uncle Joe Magliocco was a kind man.
My mother signaled to my brother that she wanted
to talk. She said, "What're we going to do with this
cetriòlo? He's behaved like an animal."

My uncle told her it wasn't her business.

"Is this the honorable family my daughter married into? She's moved six times. He doesn't help
with the kids. He doesn't go home to sleep. That
boy needs a talking to," my mother persisted. "Talk
to him. Make him behave. He can't treat my girl
like that. I want to hear a promise."

My uncle said simply, "Tomorrow, you be here,
at my house."

My mother didn't believe I should divorce Bill
or even stay separated from him. Marriage was a
sacrament for life. My mother was being very bold,
and some would say she stepped out of line by
talking to my uncle and defending me in that way.
But she knew my uncle had a soft spot in his heart
for her, and she hoped he would at least try to
persuade Bill to treat me more gently.

I was afraid Bill and my brother might turn this
into some kind of "cold war" between our families.
Now all I wanted was Bill and my children to-

gether. How had this escalated into a major family dilemma? As usual when things got hot, I yielded like the proper Mount St. Mary's alumna. I was unable to know what my best interests were or to act on them.

Now I imagined the scenario if Bill wouldn't take me back, if he spurned me when we went to my uncle's. I knew he'd take the children, then I'd die of grief. And because I could never divorce him, never remarry, never take another lover, I would wither away, living the rest of my life without sex, without hugs, without a warm body next to me in bed.

I awoke before dawn the next morning and took a long hot bath, then made myself up carefully, choosing a new shade of coral lipstick. I dressed the boys in their Sunday best. I wondered if Bill would bring Chuck with him. I pictured Chuck being pinched and squeezed by Bill's aunts and knew he had enjoyed himself, but then Chuck always did.

My family and I were sitting on lawn chairs waiting when I saw Bill's car pull up the long drive at my uncle's. My heart pounded in my ears. I stood up. When he opened the door to his car, I took a few steps forward, away from everyone else. Bill walked straight to me. He held my arms in his hands. He let go of one arm and said, "Rosalie." He let go of my other arm and said, "I think you're pregnant," and smiled. Then he walked over to Joseph and Tore. He lifted them both up together and hugged them. He shook my uncle's hand. My brother and Bill did not look at each other. The three men went into my uncle's study.

They spoke in that room for several hours. What words were said I can only guess. But I saw my brother and Bill shake hands just before I was invited to join them. Since that meeting, my husband has broken things, he has punched his fist through walls, he has even bent in half an ironing board made of iron, and broken his finger banging on a table, but he has never struck me. The rules of my husband's tradition are not all familiar to me, but I do know that once he has given his word he will never break it. I also know that when my brother and he shook hands, it didn't just mean that all was forgiven, it meant that neither of them would ever mention the conflict again. It would be as though it had never happened.

When we sat down to dinner, however, my mother had neither forgiven nor forgotten. "My daughter wants to live here," she said. "She doesn't want to go to Arizona."

I stared at my plate. I couldn't believe she was saying this. I'd never heard my mother openly confront Bill about anything until the past days. Could it be possible? Would Bill agree to stay in the East? If he did, then it would mean to me that he'd given up Erica. I'd have my husband back. I might feel more secure, which would give me back some confidence, which would make me more attractive to him, more desirable. It would mean I might be happy.

I did not dare raise my eyes, but neither did I stop my tongue from saying, "The only way I'm going back to Arizona is in a box."

CHAPTER 7

To this day I can't tell you if my husband agreed to stay because I wanted him to or because he had other reasons, reasons that had to do with his life in that other world.

Much later I learned that Bill's deciding to stay was one of the sparks that ignited a terrible war in his world. It appears that Uncle Magliocco had been having some trouble within his organization since Uncle Joe Profaci died, and some very powerful people interpreted my husband's moving into Uncle Magliocco's house as a possible alliance between their two "families." There has even been speculation that Bill and his father were trying to take over the Profaci family. Neither of these scenarios was true. Bill insists that it was really only an uncle helping out a niece and nephew.

My uncle invited us to stay in his house on Long Island until we could get settled on our own. My husband only left the grounds with my uncle occasionally, but apparently on one of those occasions my uncle asked Bill to drive him to a certain train station. When the train arrived a stranger approached and greeted Bill and my uncle, assured my uncle that everything was under control, and then Bill and my uncle came home, without Bill's asking any questions about the incident. As it turned out, people in their world interpreted my husband's presence on that day as proof that he had plotted with my uncle in a failed assassination attempt against two of the heads of other "families," Thomas Luchese and Carlo Gambino. Bill's assumed involvement meant to people in his world that Bill and his father might be trying to move in to consolidate their foothold in New York, just as other families had been trying to gain control.

When I look back on it, my uncle did seem awfully tense during those days we lived with him in his fifteen-room house. And, usually a very busy man in the outside world with his business concerns as well as on the farm, he spent most of his days at the farm and rarely went off to do business. I had never seen so many men with guns at his house before.

Although the intricacies of the politics of my husband's world fairly well escaped me, I was beginning to face facts. I was taking note. Why did members of my family often have these men with guns hanging around, keeping watch? I read things in the newspapers and was not so quick to deny their truth anymore. How could they state over and over again that the Profaci and Bonanno families were "Crime Families," members of the "Cosa Nostra," the "Mafia," "Mob," or "Syndicate" if it weren't true? As much as I would have liked to, I could no longer believe that my uncles and my father-in-law, and even my father, were the lily-white, hardworking, simple, honest, and much-maligned men I thought they were. Although this was not something I thought every day, it was something I said to myself many more times than once: My husband is a mobster, not a cowboy.

Other than the trips he went on (I'd had no idea at the time that he was traveling to Haiti and Canada, South America and Europe, and attending parties on yachts with movie stars), I had my husband home with me for weeks at a time. As far as I was concerned, my idea about moving back East to improve the quality of our life and our marriage had worked.

But even though Bill assured me it was over between him and Erica, and even though he was around more and certainly seemed more attentive than he'd been in years, I didn't trust him in the beginning, and I suppose I wanted him to make it up to me by working to get me back. And so he did.

You could even say he seduced me. He brought presents back from his trips. My favorite was a leather vest with inserts of lace. He bought me a bracelet (which I called my love bracelet) that was made of gold and had a diamond heart inlaid in it. I had the feeling he'd bought them in foreign countries or at duty-free shops in airports, but I never asked him this. The gifts weren't the only way he made up to me, though. He did exciting kinds of loving sex acts I'd never dreamed of. This made me very happy. Before, I'd always had the feeling that Bill put me on a pedestal and there were certain things he wouldn't do with me, out of respect. I tortured myself sometimes by thinking that his sex life with Erica had been wild and exotic, while his sex life with me was simply good. Now it was different. The nuns had taught me that sex was the catalyst to keeping love enforced, and that even though it was very sacred, there was no limit to the ecstasy you could feel. So, I did not feel guilty about this new kind of lovemaking; on the contrary, I was thrilled that I could give Bill such pleasure, and thankful, if a bit awed, that I could experience such pleasure myself. I have never been able to separate sex from love, so it wasn't long before the passion I felt for him in bed translated into a warmth toward him that permeated my days.

I became optimistic. Because I loved him, I wanted with all my heart for Bill to be doing things in the world I could respect. I began to have hope, and fantasies. Maybe once we left Uncle Magliocco's, Bill would work himself into a legitimate business. Maybe he'd go off to work in a suit and return every evening for dinner. Maybe we'd have a checking account; I'd start a Christmas club at the bank; we'd make out our mortgage payments in our own name. I was eager to start our new life, to begin saving for my children's colleges, so we weren't at my uncle Magliocco's very long before I became impatient to move out and into our own home where I was sure I was going to begin my happily-ever-after, at last. Bill, however, seemed to be in no hurry and urged me to be patient.

I have to admit that if it weren't for two things:

the men all over the place carrying guns, and often leaving them lying around out in the open, and the chained guard dogs, Uncle Magliocco's farm was a great place for my kids. My uncle kept horses and rode every day, sometimes swooping Chuck or Joe into the saddle of his big seventeen-hand-tall white horse. There were five acres of land, with farm animals and always some relatives or family friends to entertain them. And even the guns didn't seem too odd, since most of the men hunted with them, often bringing home a rabbit or a pheasant to throw in the sauce. Besides, although there were some men who did seem to have nothing to do but be on guard, there were others who worked. There were the vegetable gardens, the fruit trees, the flowers, the lawn, and the animals to care for.

My uncle was so heavy he had a double-sized chair made especially for himself, but fat did not mean lazy in the case of my aunt and uncle. The Maglioccos were nothing if they weren't workers. They canned tomatoes and peppers and cucuzza (Italian squash), and made tomato paste. They looked for work. They grew anything that would grow, then either cleaned and cooked it or canned it. Nothing went to waste.

I began to paint again. I loved the color of the orange and brilliant-red tomatoes and green peppers. I put them all into a bowl and painted them in oils. To my surprise, I actually duplicated their colors on the canvas. After that success I found a lot to paint on the farm.

I'm the type of person who can get into a work-

ing frenzy. If I know there's cooking or cleaning
or a project to do, I'll work and never stop until
I'm finished. When I do this people call me a real
Magliocco because everybody knows the Magliocco-
cos are workaholics. At the farm, besides keeping
up with the Maglioccos, I had my own chores to
do. Both Tore and Joseph were still in diapers, so
there was the washing and hanging; plus Chuck and
Joe were running everywhere with the son of the
caretaker and getting into everything, while Tore
was never happy unless he was riding my hip.

My husband, on the other hand, acted like a
guest. I wondered why my uncle did not expect Bill
to work on the farm like everyone else. It seemed
as though Bill and Uncle Magliocco might be in
some kind of cahoots. The gun-carrying men
seemed to respect my husband almost as much as
my uncle. In fact, maybe my husband's inactivity
bothered me more than it did anyone else, but it
didn't seem right to me that my uncle was not only
putting food in our mouths but milk in my babies'
bottles, and from what I could tell we were contributing no money. What I didn't realize then was
that my husband was doing my uncle a favor by
living in his house.

I didn't know that my uncle's organization was
under siege, that his life was in danger since the
assassination attempt against Gambino and Luchese had been discovered, and that Bill, like a good
Sicilian man, may have been putting his life on the
line for Uncle Magliocco because he was my blood
relative.

So I stepped up my "I want my own place" campaign, but Bill wasn't budging, at least not until one morning when my little Joe wandered away from the breakfast table, found a shotgun leaning against a wall in the living room, and shot it off.

We heard the explosion. I flew out of my chair and into the living room. There was Joe, standing in a corner of the room, stunned. I'll never forget the way he looked, so tiny in that large room, standing there in his red pajamas. He was so frail, he looked more like a one-year-old than a kid of two and a half. The shotgun was at his feet, and only when I hugged him did I notice the gaping hole above me in the ceiling. I began to cry. Joseph began to cry. My uncle came trundling down the stairs yelling, and men came running into the house with rifles and guns in their hands. I pushed Joseph's face into my neck and looked for Bill. He had Chuck in his arms. He picked up the gun at our feet and shoved it at one of the men. He said, "Jesus Christ, get this out of my sight. Why do you guys have to leave this shit laying around here?"

I could hear Tore crying from his high chair in the kitchen. My aunt ran to him as my uncle, breathless and holding his chest, collapsed into his double-sized chair. "He all right, Ro?" he said.

I wiped the tears from my face with the sleeve of my robe and nodded as I rocked Joseph in my arms.

"Well, I'm not," he said. "Come on, somebody clean up the mess," he ordered his men.

I vowed that my husband might be a mobster,

he might carry a gun, but there would never be one lying around *my* house.

Bill took Joe from my arms so that he held Chuck on one side of him and Joe on the other. "Come on, boys," he said to distract them, "let's go see some horses."

I would later learn that my uncle had been so concerned about his life's being in danger that he'd asked a local mechanic to install a type of starter in his car so that he could start it up from inside the house. At the time I had no idea how that shot-gun blast must have scared the poor man half to death.

In fact, Uncle Magliocco would die of a heart attack in little over a month.

I can never be certain what motivates my husband, and it is not my place to ask. In our tradition the man makes all decisions. He is like God. But a couple of weeks after Joseph shot off the gun, Bill took me and the kids for a ride on a Sunday, parked the car in front of a house in East Meadow, Long Island, and said, "You wanted a house. There it is." He nodded toward a ranch-style house that looked nice enough. But I had to stop myself from crying by an act of will; would I never even be allowed to choose my own home?

In my anger and disappointment, I could see only the house's faults, which were three-fold: It was near a corner, in addition to being on a street much too busy for the safe and comfortable raising of kids, and it had a pool. This pool was built-in and took up practically the entire backyard.

As I trudged, more than walked, through the house, my body feeling heavier than usual—I was six months' pregnant now—I grumbled something about having to be on top of the kids every minute worrying about that stupid pool.

"Jesus Christ," Bill said. "She's never happy. Always the martyr. Life's so hard. You know how many people would die for a pool?"

He had it boarded over and we settled into our new house. As positive as I was that I was carrying a daughter, I restrained myself from decorating her room with pinks and frills until she was born. On March 8, when I had my only daughter and last baby, I had such a sense of well-being, such a feeling of optimism, that I was positive our life in our new house, beginning with this beautiful new baby, our daughter, was going to be good from now on. We named her Filippa after Bill's mother, just changing the spelling of her dead sister's name, and Bill fell in love with her in a way he'd never fallen for his sons. He invited everyone over to show her off and began to call her Gigi, after the film by the same name that was popular at the time. It had the song "Thank Heaven for Little Girls" in it. The name stuck, and to this day everyone calls her Gigi.

I complained that Gigi had no clothes, and a truck arrived the next day filled with them. Soon after, a Progresso truck arrived filled with canned foods to store in the basement. So strong was my feeling of optimism that I wasn't suspicious about where all these goods or the money to pay for them had come from. I didn't worry when Bill bought me a new car either. I was happy. He was being a good provider, so I felt secure, and I had three wonderful boys and now a beautiful daughter, and a husband whom I had fallen in love with all over again.

Now that my family was complete, I began to make long-range plans. I'd always believed in setting goals, and I decided that as soon as Gigi was old enough, I would travel into the city and attend the Fashion Institute of Technology. My goal was to become a dress designer. I'd made up my mind that I needed a career, and that if I were going to be working, it had best be at something I enjoyed. Over the years I'd observed that I was truly happy when being creative—redoing a piece of furniture, sewing a dress, or painting a design on something— and losing myself in my work. I needed an outlet for my artistic side, and since I loved clothes and admired true craftsmanship, it seemed that to be a dress designer would be just the thing. I also knew myself well enough to predict that if I had to be submissive to a boss, or work under a man as his secretary, say, I would not be happy.

Maybe I got the idea from my mother that to be truly happy or fulfilled I should have a career. My mother never came out and said this to me, but she always praised and most admired the women who had careers. In fact, she'd seemed in awe of them. I did not at all think that working would detract from motherhood, which was and always would be of the most importance to me. I figured working would make me happy, and if I were happy, I'd be a better mother.

I didn't say any of this to Bill, though. In fact, I was saying less and less to Bill because he'd become awfully busy. Every morning he got dressed in a suit and left. When I began to ask him where he was going he would respond in one of two ways. He would either tell me it was none of my business, or he'd tell me exactly where in Brooklyn or Manhattan he was off to, which, as he knew, meant exactly nothing to me. It was in the late summer of 1964, four or five months after I had Gigi and a while since Bill had begun to go everywhere with a man named Carl, when I began to suspect that Carl was Bill's bodyguard and that my darling husband was dressing up and going off to be a gangster every day. I pictured him standing on street corners and lounging around in clubs, leaning back in a chair pulling on a cigar, talking and joking with other men who were doing the same thing. I didn't like the picture one bit. I had no respect for this, and above all I wanted, I really wanted, to be able to respect my husband and the father of my children.

Then, in September, my husband received news that a grand jury was acting on information it received from the 1963 Senate hearings on organized crime and had a subpoena in Bill's name. Among other things, a man named Joseph Valachi had testified that Mr. Bonanno, an alleged "boss" of one of five New York "Families," had been his sponsor.

My husband disappeared, along with any remaining trace of my dreams for a happily-ever-after.

CHAPTER 8

A disappearing husband has become a staple of my life, a fact I have never gotten used to. My husband would say it was necessary that I not be informed of his disappearances because then when the FBI, or whoever else wanted to know, came to ask me— the worst liar on the face of the earth—where my husband went, I would have no idea. Bill liked to say, "Women have big mouths. They can't keep anything to themselves." I suppose this is why my husband's world, where silence is a virtue as well as a necessity, has been and always will be fraternal. I had nothing to tell the FBI when they came to ask where my husband went.

Had I been a different type of person, more attuned to these things, more aware and not so practiced in the art of denial, I would have guessed that my husband was about to fly the coop. He'd been giving me more money than I needed lately, telling me to save it for a rainy day. In his way he'd been encouraging me to build a nest egg.

When he first left, though, I had no idea where my husband had gone or for how long. So when the FBI came, I told the agents I didn't know anything.

Occasionally one of Bill's men would drop by and tell me to go to such and such a phone booth at such and such a time, then I'd arrange for a baby-sitter and travel to the phone booth. The farthest I traveled was to a phone in Macy's in Roosevelt Field. I'd answer the phone at exactly the time Bill's friend had told me to, and there Bill's voice would be on the other end of the line. He never gave me any information, but, then, I never asked. He could have been around the corner watching me as I spoke or in Texas for all I knew. We talked about the kids and my main concern, which was money. What would happen when it was gone? He told me not to worry. He asked, "Have you ever been without?" I couldn't point to a time, but it certainly felt like I had. I had cause to worry about it plenty, since Bill was the one who had it in his pocket and I was the one with my palm perpetually open.

It was a little over a month since Bill had disappeared. The weather had taken on a chill and one day it was winter. I turned on the evening news to hear that Bill's father had been kidnapped as he was walking on Park Avenue with his lawyer. There was speculation that Mr. Bonanno had been assassinated.

Kidnapped. Assassinated. How could these words be in my life? How could they be applied to my family? I sat on the sofa and said a silent prayer for Bill's father. I hoped that one of Bill's men would be by to reassure me somehow. Now, for the first time since he disappeared, I couldn't help asking myself real questions: Where was my husband? Was his life in danger? What did he have to do with all this? If my father-in-law had been murdered, did that put me and my children in danger? Surely if we were, Bill would somehow protect us. Wouldn't he?

I sat on the sofa, stunned. Chuck had made a paper airplane and was making it dip and soar with his hand as Joe chased him around the room, crying and reaching for the plane, which Chuck held forever out of his grasp. Tore chased behind too, but instead of crying he was laughing and clapping and jumping. Gigi sat in her playpen arranging her toys in one corner. A wave of self-pity washed over me. A normal husband would be returning from work about now. The kids would race to him and he'd muss up their hair and lift them high and make a paper plane for Joseph to stop his crying. Gigi was only seven months old. She'd learned to sit up by herself and to hold her own bottle since her father last saw her. My eyes had begun to swell with tears before I stopped myself. I needed to be strong. I needed to put this all aside. If I needed to worry, I could do it alone, at night. For now, I vowed, I would make life normal for my children. I would be consistent if nothing else. They'd have nutritious breakfasts, lunches, and dinners, served at the same time every day. Their house would be clean and orderly, their clothes neat, their faces and hands clean. They would join Little League and Boy Scouts. We would go to church every Sunday. These things, at least, were in my power.

"Why don't you let your brother play with the plane?" I suggested to Chuck.

He gave it to Joseph, then Tore had a fit and tried to pull one of Gigi's rattles through the mesh of the playpen, which got her going. All was normal with my children. This gave me comfort. I thanked God.

The next morning when I opened the door to send Chuck off to the first grade, I was bombarded by a crowd of people yelling, "Mrs. Bonanno, Mrs. Bonanno." Cameras were clicking, TV crews jostling for advantage. I pulled Chuck back in and shut the door.

Chuck looked at me in his calm, curious way. I didn't know what to say. "They don't know where Grandpa or Daddy is and they've come to ask us."

"Oh," he said.

I figured a refresher course on silence, one that his father had given the children, was in order. "Remember what Daddy said. If anybody asks you anything, just tell them you don't know or tell them to come and ask your mother. Okay?"

He nodded and I walked him out to the sidewalk, where he went on his way to school.

The circus did not leave my front lawn, and the telephone did not stop ringing all day. I had no comment. Always. I knew nothing.

When Chuck came home he told me he'd been pulled out of class to talk to a man in a room. The man had asked him if he knew where his father was.

"What did you say?" I asked him.

"Nothing."

"That's all he asked?"

"Yes."

Joseph said a man asked him questions too.

"What?" I asked Joseph.

"He asked me when."

"When what?"

"*When* Daddy was home."

"What did you say?"

"Yesterday."

"Was Daddy home yesterday?" I asked him to see if he understood what *yesterday* meant, or if he had purposely lied, which I would not have liked.

"Yes," he said.

"You did fine, Joseph." I kissed him on the cheek.

That night, I tidied, scoured, and mopped until at last I was tired enough to sleep.

Now there was no more driving to Macy's for phone calls from Bill. My mother came to visit and help. She played with the kids and pitched in with the housework. She made a pot of soup, some for dinner and some to freeze for later. Of my husband and my father-in-law she said nothing, except "God help them," followed by "But with them you never know. You never know." Some neighbors offered sympathy when I ran into them at the store or the pediatrician's office. My cousins, who I'd hoped would visit once I'd moved into my new home, were busy with their own children and lived in Brooklyn or on Staten Island, which was quite a trip with a car full of little ones. Still, with all this publicity and attention, I had to wonder if they'd have ventured into my house had I lived next door.

My one relief from the tedium of being alone was visits from an older distant cousin named Nellie. She lived four towns away on Long Island. Nellie was full of love and advice. When I tried to complain to her about my life, she told me to keep a smiling face and my opinions to myself. "Lookit, honey, you can get more with sugar. Flattery will get you everywhere. These people [people in your husband's world], if you're going to be on any side of them, you better be on their good side. In other words, Rosalie, be a little tactful, cunning, and suave. Life with your type of man could be easier if you were more diplomatic. You have to make him think it's his idea." It was from her that I learned what a "kiss-up type person" was and that these qualities even existed.

Aside from the visits with Nellie, I was lonely. I was frightened. But my days were busy with the kids and housework and the effort of not thinking. The nights were different. I prayed for Bill's safety, for his father's soul, and for the strength to raise my children alone. I kept reminding myself that I did have the three ingredients for happiness: something to love, something to do, and something to hope for. So I continued to concentrate on my blessings to overcome my fear. And I continued to pray.

My prayers were answered.

In the first week of November I received a letter

from Bill. It was postmarked Bennington, Vermont. It said:

My Dearest Rosalie,

I know by this time you must be worried sick because I haven't been in touch with you.

First, no matter what you hear about me, as of this moment I am well. Please do not be influenced by what anyone tells you about me. I can't begin to explain why I can not see you right now, but I hope that some day we'll be able to get together.

I trust the boys are fine. I hope Joseph has not had any more trouble with his chest. I'll bet Salvatore must be unmanageable; he is at the age that can give you plenty of trouble. I've been wondering if Chuckie likes school any better than he did.

I miss seeing Gigi; she must be a doll by now. I'll bet she has grown a lot. It seems an eternity since I saw her last.

I realize that all this trouble I am now having must be a strain on you. However, I now thank God that I never discussed with you my personal affairs. Believe me, you are better off this way. Keep your chin up.

Use whatever money you need from what we had put away. Try to make it last as long as possible because I do not know how long I'll be away.

Rosalie, don't expect to hear from me for some time. Please don't worry. You know I

can't call so please don't worry about me.
Stay well, take care of the children, occupy
yourself with them. Pay no attention to what
anyone tells you. Kiss the kids.
   All my love always,
   Bill

I did kiss the kids, and then suppressed the urge
to call my mother and tell her the good news that
my husband was still alive, because surely the
phone was unsafe. I realized that Bill had said nothing about his father and wondered if my father-in-
law were indeed dead.

I had heard nothing from my mother-in-law during
all this time; not that I had expected to, considering
the problem with using phones. I had wondered
about her sometimes as I lay in bed. I wondered
how she coped with the not knowing. I wondered if
she cried when she was alone, if she resented her
husband for the life he'd led her into. Somehow,
even before I learned some things about her life, I
doubted it.

Many years later, after all that happened that fall
had become public record, I found out something
very few people knew, something that my mother-
in-law took with her to the grave, but that my husband told me after she died, by way of illustrating
the strength of some women—the women from that
other generation who came from Sicily and had
grown up with and remained close to the tradition.

My father-in-law had truly been kidnapped, and

it was as much of a shock to my husband as to everyone else. But because my husband didn't know who had done it or if his father were alive or dead, he and his men "took to the mattresses," which is a way of saying they went into hiding, sleeping here and there in various apartments set up for that purpose. They kept moving so nobody could pin them down, sometimes driving up to New England, then back again.

But before Bill left, in fact immediately after he heard on the news, like everyone else, that his father had been kidnapped, he went to his aunt's house in Brooklyn where his mother had been staying and pirated his mother six blocks away just before the FBI showed up at his aunt's door with subpoenas. He made some arrangements, and then the following night he went back to get his mother, who knew better than to ask questions. She simply followed her son's directions, which were "Lie down on the backseat." He covered her with a blanket, then drove her to another relative's house in New Jersey, where my mother-in-law lived for three months in a basement room, sort of like Anne Frank had lived in an attic. The only time she could make noise or venture from the room was after the children had left for school, but when they returned at three in the afternoon she had to stay perfectly still until they left again the next morning. Weekends were hell.

While Bill was still in hiding himself he did manage a couple of visits to his mother in the basement to see how things were going. When he visited he was sometimes unkempt and always obviously under a lot of pressure. His mother never voiced a complaint. She never even asked when her ordeal would be over. Nor did she ask about Bill's father, knowing that if Bill could answer he would have told her. All she ever said was, "What can I do to help?"

I admire that woman. Her strength. Her courage. Her devotion. Perhaps I could never emulate it because I was born here in America and of a different generation. I know my husband has seen my lack of understanding, my complaining, my desire for a kind of life he could never give me as a character fault, an inherent weakness. That I never was and never could be the type of wife for him that his mother had been for his father was a continual disappointment to Bill. I understood this and wondered if he understood that just as disappointing to me was his inability to be just a regular, calm, and neutral guy instead of always at the center of a storm.

On Christmas that year I received a telegram and flowers. They were from Bill. The telegram said, simply, "Merry Christmas. Kiss the kids. I love you."

The children and I spent the holiday at my mother's and the conversation tactfully steered away from my home life. I'd dressed the boys up in navy blue blazers and Gigi in a red velvet dress with white tights and a bow in her hair. I wished Bill could have seen them. He would have made a fuss over Gigi, I knew. The boys would have clamored around him, jockeying for position on his lap. I tried with all my might not to feel self-pity or bitterness. I tried to think of all I had to be thankful for. I had these beautiful children and my family nearby, and I'd been frugal enough to buy presents, though my funds were dwindling.

On New Year's Eve I stayed out on Long Island instead of going into Brooklyn to be with my family. After the children were in bed, I was exhausted as usual, but I planned to force myself to stay up and watch the ball drop over Times Square on my television. It was the beginning of a New Year, after all, and I really would feel like a pathetic lonely old lady at twenty-eight if I didn't welcome it with my eyes open. I'd poured myself a glass of champagne and had just settled into the corner of the couch after turning on the TV when I heard that Bill Bonanno, the son of Joseph Bonanno, had been arrested in Tucson, Arizona.

I expect that most women hearing that their husband had just been arrested might be worried, might be angry, might be sad. Not me. I was overjoyed. This meant he would be coming home . . . to face a trial. Not only did I know where my husband was, but for once in my life I knew what he was up to on New Year's.

CHAPTER 9

BACK in December Bill received a phone call at a telephone booth, in which a strange man's voice told him his father was living and safe. My husband then called his father's lawyer to tell him the news, and the lawyer, who I suppose should have known better, let the news out. A New York judge put a material witness warrant out on Bill. After they caught up with him in Tucson on New Year's Eve, they transported him back to New York and held him on a twenty-five-thousand-dollar bond and ordered him to appear in court to testify about his father's disappearance.

During the three months he appeared before the grand jury, he was picked up at our house every morning by his lawyer, who lived nearby. This meant that Bill shaved and dressed in his suit and sat at the breakfast table with the family, his after-shave sweetening the air, his presence calming the children, then left, often kissing me on the cheek. This time I wasn't kidding myself into thinking his presence at breakfast before going to court was anything like a typical happy family life, but it was nice. He came home nearly every night. The children were happy. Gigi had just turned one and Bill had gone crazy buying her stuffed animals. And I have to confess to a certain fantasy: that Bill was the lawyer he'd set out to be instead of the witness. Then Bill's lawyer called one afternoon and informed me that Bill wouldn't be home for dinner. He was going to jail. The witness had become a prisoner because he refused to talk.

The government wanted him to repeat exactly what he'd told his father's lawyer on the phone the day he'd heard that his father was alive and well. My husband argued that due to lawyer-client confidentiality, he was not obliged to tell the grand jury any such thing. The government argued that the confidentiality wasn't operative because the lawyer wasn't Bill's but his father's, and the government won.

It was early in March and unseasonably warm. The sun was still bright even though it was four o'clock, and I'd opened some windows. Now I sat on the sofa, hearing the shouts of my boys in the backyard and watching Gigi drag her telephone by the cord. The lawyer had said it was possible that Bill could be in jail for more than a year, although he doubted it would go on that long. I put Gigi's jacket on and set her on the lawn with her brothers and sat on the back stoop. I was angry.

When I went to visit Bill at the Federal House of Detention on West Street in Manhattan, I think I was in shock. The room was crowded and noisy, and I had to speak to Bill through a telephone while I watched his face behind a dirty glass partition. I was embarrassed and humiliated and I remembered for a moment the marble floors and high ceilings of the convent school, and thought of where life had taken me.

Seeing Bill dressed in prison clothes, talking slowly into the phone, my big, proud, burly, and brusque husband looking so humble and so sad, was enough to break my heart. The words he spoke, however, did not match his restrained tone. He told me he wanted me to bring the children to see him. He said, "I want them to see me in jail. I have no regrets. I don't lower my eyes to anyone because I'm here doing what I think is the right thing to do." He said he wanted our children to know everything there was to know about him, so that later on they could never look at Bill and say, "You lied to me." He wanted to set an example, to show them that because he believed in something strongly he was willing to sacrifice his life for that belief. We would not lie to our children about their father, as so many of the people Bill knew had, telling their children their father had gone to college or was off to the army, when really he was in jail.

Each week I brought a different boy. Gigi, I reasoned, was too young. Before Bill had left we'd hired a Colombian woman named Elisa, who spoke little English, to help me with the children and the housework. I left the children with her each time I went to visit. I think it was Joseph who asked me why Daddy lived in a telephone booth.

I always tried to bring home a treat, a Tootsie Roll pop or Cracker Jacks, to the kids who stayed behind because they felt so left out and lonely for their father. I always told them their father had asked for them and said they should mind their mother, but invariably before I got all the words out of my mouth they'd be chiming, "I want to go next."

"No, me."

"No, me."

I realized how much they loved their father, and what a good father Bill was. He taught them things and treated them less like little children than like young adults. He gave them tasks he knew they could accomplish, then would congratulate them for a job well done to build their confidence. Even though he was the disciplinarian, the parent with the booming voice who quieted them as we sat down to dinner or piled into the car for a ride, they never resented getting yelled at or disciplined by him. I would even go so far as to say they were a bit in awe of Bill.

Finally, in June, I came home from grocery shopping, and the housekeeper, who knew nothing about our private life, said, "Your husband called and said he'd be home for dinner." For mysterious reasons, Bill and his lawyer and whoever else he'd consulted with—I'd learned by now that any decision having to do with that world seemed to be made by committee—decided it was okay to repeat the conversation he'd had with the man in the telephone booth concerning his father, thereby purging himself of contempt of court and setting himself free.

I wanted to kiss Elisa, but she was a rather reserved person, so I just dropped the groceries on the counter and ran to the phone. I called my mother first and then about twelve other relatives and friends, then ran back to the store to buy more food for the celebratory dinner.

To my horror Bill was not at all humble or contrite, or acting grateful for his freedom. In a way he acted like the whole experience had been a big joke. He was the life of the party, shamelessly describing people he'd met in prison, recounting the food he'd eaten, his daily routine. I blushed from embarrassment as I served the food. I hid in the kitchen, pretending to still be cooking to avoid looking in anyone's eyes.

Bill's shamelessness about his life in jail and my embarrassment and silent disapproval became a constant subtle undercurrent in our marriage. Now Bill carried a pistol and made no attempt to hide the fact from our children. When Chuck asked him why, he said, "Someone might want to harm Daddy and this will discourage him."

When he wasn't wearing his pistol in a shoulder holster, he put it on top of the bureau, and the kids were instructed that the top of his bureau was forbidden terrain and that they were never, under any circumstances, ever to touch anything on it. I have to admit I used the rule to advantage. If the kids were fighting over a toy, I'd threaten them, "If you don't stop, I'll put it on Daddy's bureau."

I hated guns. I was determined that my children were not going to follow in their father's footsteps.

I don't think Bill ever would have encouraged them to do so, but neither would he have discouraged them. He was adamant about some things: Snitching was unqualifiedly forbidden. When one of the kids forgot and told on his brother, then he was the one who was admonished, not the offending brother. I had my rules too. One was: no toy guns. When a friend brought a toy gun over one day, I threw it straight into the garbage over the protests of my children. When Bill came home, he found the gun there and yelled at me for throwing a perfectly good toy like that away. I did not retrieve the toy, and neither did Bill.

In the fall of 1965, when Chuck went back to school, repeating the first grade because his reading had been so poor—even though he was excellent with numbers and anything that involved constructing something with his two hands—he had to answer the following question on a form: "What does your father do for a living?" He answered, "Drives a truck." Chuck got that idea from the fact that his father had become partners in a warehouse in Brooklyn with a man named Hank Perrone. Bill got a kick out of Chuck's response to the question. I didn't think it was so funny.

Now, whenever Bill came home, a man named Hank was with him more than half the time. Whatever my husband was up to, he was very busy.

When Bill was home we were tense with each other, but it wasn't the kind of tension that comes from fear or anger or frustration. It was more sexual in nature. In a way, I guess, I just got excited when he was around. I always knew when he was looking at me, even if I had my back turned. Our lovemaking was sporadic but extremely enjoyable. There were mornings when it was hard for me to leave our bed. But underlying all our feelings of tension or love were hopes we both held on to fiercely. His was that I would become the kind of wife who would love and accept him unconditionally. Mine was that my husband would change and provide me with a normal life. I think we were both waiting for the change in the other person to occur, and not knowing exactly when this might happen kept us hooked into each other and off balance.

This was a social time. Bill had a lot of new friends in New York whom he often brought to dinner at the spur of the moment. He would call from the city and say, "I'll be home with twelve people in an hour," and, one way or another, dinner was ready when they arrived. Then Bill would put his arm around me and say, "That's my Rosalie. Do you believe her?" Saturday nights, sometimes we'd have parties, and then the men brought their wives. They were a lively crew. Sometimes the volume would get so high—and I'm not talking just about the music—I'd be afraid we were disturbing the neighbors. Bill had all the Mario Lanza, Jerry Vale, and Al Martino records and people enjoyed his hi-fi. My husband always seemed to be the center of attention at these parties. Everyone flocked around him and it was as though he were the apex of activity. I had no question that my husband, in some capacity, was the leader of these men, but that didn't stop Hank's wife, Frances, from teasing him every chance she got. I liked Frances best of all. She had a very loud voice and could swear like a sailor, but she also had a wonderful sense of humor, a cute figure, and an outrageously poufed and teased and high-in-the-sky hairdo. I think Frances was the bluntest woman I've ever known. We became friends independently of our husbands. And when she came over one day for a visit and our kids were off playing, giving us a breather to talk in the kitchen, I complained that I wished Bill would pay more attention to me. The reason was because I would have liked him never to take his eyes off me, although I didn't admit this to Frances.

She said, "Well, Rosalie, no offense, but, I mean, I like this about you, but you are kinda like a nun."

"What do you mean?" I couldn't believe my ears because I felt very much like a wife and mother and nothing at all like a nun.

"Did you ever think of dressing sexy, for instance? I mean, it's not a sin, you know. I don't know what they taught you in them Catholic schools, but they're not gonna send you to hell for it."

I had never heard the word *sex* used in that context before. Had I somehow blocked it out because I hadn't understood it? Sex I'd thought of as an act. What did *sexy* mean? But how could I admit my ignorance to Frances? I wanted her to be my friend. Instead I said, "How do you mean?"

"Something a little low-cut." She cupped her

breasts in her hands. "A little tight across the ass."
She wiggled her rear end and made her eyes go
wide. "It wouldn't hurt to wear a little more
makeup. Maybe you should be a blonde. You
could, you know. You got light enough skin. Yeah.
A blonde. What a surprise. Believe me, he'll drop
dead. You're a pretty girl. You should flaunt it. I
got the feeling with you that you been hiding in a
closet for ten years."

I took Frances's advice. I bleached my hair, and
started going to the beauty salon almost on a
weekly basis, where they teased my newly blond
hair into a bouffant hairdo. I wore eyebrow pencil
and blush. I made myself a couple of sheath
dresses, which I wore for entertaining. I copied Frances's style and took to wearing tight pants with
high heels.

In my naïveté I concluded that it worked, because Bill took me with him on one of his trips to
Haiti. We stayed in a luxurious hotel, and when we
went to the casino in the evenings, Bill proudly
guided me around, and for the first time since my
wedding I felt like royalty. Everyone knew Bill,
everyone greeted us. People stared. This made me
feel very uncomfortable. For one thing, I knew I'd
stepped into a part of his world that had been secret
from me. Obviously he'd been here often. Obviously he had something to do with the business of
this place. Maybe he was even an owner. And the
women were unsettling. They were beautiful for
one thing, and when we passed they smiled and
nodded to Bill, then gave me the once-over. How

many of them had he been with? I forced the question from my mind and concentrated on feeling guilty instead of jealous. I'd left my children to carouse in casinos in foreign countries. Surely this could not be right. I returned after four days, convinced I could be sexy and even a little glamorous, but not convinced at all that I wanted to be that way outside of our house.

Since his father's disappearance, Bill had never mentioned him to me and I had never asked. One day Bill came home from a trip wearing a sport jacket I was sure had belonged to his father. I decided that what I'd thought all along—that his father was really dead—was definitely true. My husband and his father were very close, and sometimes through the years I'd wondered how much choice Bill had actually been offered in his life. He had a great love and absolute respect for his father. He would do anything his father asked him. I wondered if Bill had first become really entrenched in his father's world after the Apalachin fiasco, when his father had needed Bill's assistance so badly. Bill had been in school then. What if Apalachin had never happened? Might Bill have become a lawyer after all? I wondered if his father's dying would free my husband to go straight. Maybe Bill was mostly legitimate anyway. It was possible. He had that warehouse, land in Arizona, it seemed he had that casino, and maybe he had other businesses and other places to which he had to travel. But still, why the bodyguard? Why all the male companions? I gave up thinking about it. Occasionally the Bonanno name appeared in the papers, and then I did my best to ignore it.

And I succeeded. Until the first days of February 1966. One Friday night at the end of January, Bill called from a telephone booth and told me that no matter what I read in the newspapers or heard on the radio or saw on television, he was fine and that I wasn't to worry. I said, "You're not coming home?"

He said, "Rosalie," in an exhausted yet indulgent voice that said to me, "Don't you know better than to ask that question?"

Bill sounded very strange on the phone. There was a lot of breath in his voice, as though he had been running. I was afraid for him. He did not come home. There was nothing in the newspaper, but I heard on the radio that there had been a "Mafia-style" shootout on Troutman Street in Brooklyn. I wondered if Bill had done the shooting or had been the one being shot at. I didn't know which scenario I preferred.

On Monday Bill came home. He was with four men, including Hank and Carl. They seemed strangely jubilant. Almost excited. It was as though their cheerfulness were forced, as though they were playacting, but I didn't see why they would do this for my benefit. I wondered if they were doing it for each other, to keep their spirits up. Or if they actually relished danger. They were carrying newspapers and glued themselves to the TV. Although the other men came and went, but mostly stayed,

Joseph and Fay Bonanno's wedding picture. My father was an usher. The inscription reads: "To my dear friend Salvatore. All my friendship with affection, Joseph." My father is at the far right. (*Ferrantino Studio*)

My baptism.

Me at three.

Me with my brothers, Sal and Frank, and my sister, Antoinette, in 1943. I was already going to boarding school.

At the shore. Me, my mother, and my father in his favorite nautical whites.

My First Communion, with Sister Mary Francis at Mount St. Mary.

Me at ten, and Bill at thirteen (*Caesar Passarelli*). I was already in love with him.

At a wedding with my parents. Me, peeking out second from left. Next, my mother, my father, and Fay and Joe Bonanno.

My confirmation. Mrs. Bonanno was my godmother. I was eleven.

My father in his New York real estate office.

Me at thirteen, with Uncle
Joe Magliocco on a trip.

Mount St. Mary.

Visitation Academy, winter uniform. I am in the middle of the
front row.

My mother and father.

Brother Sal's graduation ball from New York Military Academy. Sal is third from right, and I am beside him, on the right. Catherine, my best friend and sister-in-law to be, is on the extreme left. (*Don Donato*)

Bill and me, on my first visit to Tucson. I'm seventeen and Bill is falling in love with me at last.

High school graduation, Mount St. Mary. I am second from right, first row. (*Don Donato*)

Yearbook picture. "Roe . . . charm of a quiet personality." (*Don Donato*)

Wedding invitation.

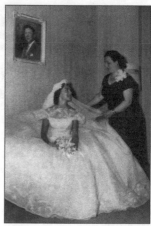

Mama and me just before the wedding. Papa's picture is on the wall. He died two years earlier. (*Ida Art Studios*)

From the altar as man and wife. (*Ida Art Studios*)

Wedding reception at the Sheraton Astor Hotel in Times Square.
(*Ida Art Studios*)

Honeymoon in Paris at the Lido.

Easter morning in Flagstaff, Arizona. Notice the snow and icicles.

Joseph Bonanno raises a toast. I'm pregnant with the baby I lost.

Chuck with his bear, made famous in the film of *Honor Thy Father*.

New York winter, Chuck and Joe.

My godfather, Uncle Magliocco, with his white horse.

Gigi's first birthday, Tore's second. Standing, from left, Aunt Marion, Mama, and me. Sitting, from left, Joe, four, Gigi, Tore, and Chuck, seven. (*Paul Aniess*)

My sister's wedding. Chuck was ring bearer; I was maid of honor. (*Ida Art Studios*)

Our children.

Bill feeding me a drink in our busy household in East Meadow, Long Island.

Two of the men who lived with us. That's me by the stove.

In San Jose, California. Bill cooking a traditional goat on Easter Sunday.

Bill and me in the California sunshine.

My thirty-ninth birthday.

Chuck at seventeen on his uni-ski invention. Notice he has both feet on one ski.

Gigi skis in Tahoe.

Our teenagers, ages thirteen to nineteen. Mom's the smallest one!

Me as a career woman.

Bill and me in Mexico, where I fell in love all over again.

Our family. Bill back from Mexico, the kids in from college.
Top, from left, Chuck, Joe, Tore.

Joe's graduation from medical school.
With me and my mother.

Bill, master chef.

With his brothers, Chuck and Joe.

Tore's graduation from the University of Arizona.

With Bill and me.

Mother of the bride.

Bill holding his grandson, with his father, Joseph Bonanno, and his son, young Dr. Joe.

Bill did not leave the house for several days. I resisted reading any papers or listening to the news, but on Wednesday I relented. If my husband were in danger, I should know. The Wednesday *Times* said:

> The humble Ridgewood district of Brooklyn where Joseph (Joe Banannas) Bonanno began his climb to power in the Mafia many years ago was under close police scrutiny yesterday as a sequel to Friday night's shooting spree in Troutman Street.
>
> Detectives are investigating the possibility that the gun battle—in which more than 20 shots were fired, apparently without hitting anyone—was an incident of the intra-Mafia struggle over a successor to Bonanno as head of the underworld "family" bearing his name. Bonanno has been missing since the eve of October, 1964. . . .
>
> A report that spread through the underworld yesterday was that one faction had tried to kill Salvatore (Bill) Bonanno, son of the missing chieftain, or to scare him from wielding what influence he might have in the selection of his father's successor.

I didn't understand the seeming jubilation of Bill and the men. This shootout had happened the night Bill phoned to tell me he was fine. Obviously he had been at Troutman Street and the paper was

probably accurate in reporting that someone or
many people had tried to kill him.

I stuffed the paper in the trash. I wished I hadn't
read it. If someone had tried to shoot Bill this time,
had Bill shot people other times? I really didn't
want to know. I was glad he kept his life from me.
I was thankful.

I did not know at the time that, contrary to the
wishes of some of the men in my husband's world,
my husband had assumed the role of *consigliere* to
his father. This was seen as nepotism and highly
unusual because Bill was so young and because a
consigliere traditionally is a kind of sounding board
or counselor to the father of the "family." How
could a son counsel a father, they reasoned, and
appointed a man named Gasper Di Gregano as the
head of the Bonanno family. This created a schism
within the family. Some of the people sided with
Di Gregario and some with Bill. The night Bill was
ambushed, he had been on his way to a meeting
with Di Gregario.

I did not want my husband to be shot at. I did
not want my husband to be shooting people. I kept
myself busy and never questioned, even to myself,
what my husband did when he left the house.

When his father showed up three months later—
not only alive but fit and trim and tanned—and
turned himself in to the U.S. Federal District Court
at Foley Square, he was let out on bail with the
limitation that he must live in the southern or east-

ern district of New York, which meant at my house.

Now there was no escaping my husband's world or the war between the factions that remained loyal and those that defected.

CHAPTER 10

I have always held a high respect for my father-in-law. He is an extremely intelligent man with a lot of charisma that translates into a powerful presence. By this I mean that if Mr. Bonanno is in a room, all eyes are on him. They can't help but be. My father-in-law has rarely criticized me or lost his temper with me, yet in his presence I've always felt that I'm being judged, that he's watching every move I make, and that the judgment is that I don't deserve any medals. Mr. Bonanno possesses a tremendous amount of dignity. He is not the type of man I could appear in front of wearing my bathrobe, even if it were the break of dawn. Now that he was living in my house, I never left my bedroom at any time of day or night without my hair in place and my stockings on. Shy to begin with, I was afraid to open my mouth for fear I'd be judged stupid. But my father-in-law's daily presence in my life was only part of my problem.

This time I wasn't suffering from neglect or loneliness or another woman. This time it was the constant presence of men. My life was so full of them that there were times I considered running off to a convent. My father-in-law came with his bodyguard Pete, who slept in the basement with my husband's bodyguard Carl, and sometimes Hank as well, and at other times even more men. When the whole crew was staying over, the snoring sounded like a horn symphony straining up the stairs from the basement. It kept me and the children awake, while my husband, the consummate warrior, could concentrate his energies on sleeping soundly just as he could concentrate his energies on remaining ever alert.

To put it plainly, this time of my life was a waking nightmare. This was the routine of my days: Up with the kids, dressing, breakfasting, washing faces. Then I brought Chuck to a parochial school, Joe to a private school because he was ready to go and his age didn't allow him to enroll in public school yet, and Tore to a Montessori school. Back home. Breakfast for Bill's father, Bill if he was there, which he often was not, the bodyguards, and any other othernight guests. Dishes. Laundry, which was a never-shrinking mountain of sheets and towels in the basement. Lunch, again for assorted men. Then I fed my father-in-law and the kids at six, and inevitably had to feed another batch of men later. Then, later still, others for coffee.

Most evenings there would be fifteen or sixteen people over. I served vegetables on huge platters that were made for pasta. I couldn't be very creative in my cooking because my father-in-law wanted to eat what he already knew. We had an antipasto, pasta, meat and vegetables, salad, fruit, coffee, and cake every day. On Sundays we had perciatelli pasta with plain sauce followed by a leg of lamb or a meat or chicken dish and vegetables. These days were called my seven-course Sundays and I'd be in the kitchen at least ten hours. I rarely made meatballs anymore, because once Mr. Bonanno learned that fat wasn't good for him, he stopped eating meat sauce.

My father-in-law and my husband were always having meetings in Mr. Bonanno's room, where a cloud of cigar smoke would escape through the door whenever it opened. Men came and went all day. They were plotting things, I suspected. The Bonanno name was constantly in the papers and on TV and radio, which droned on in the background all day long. The constant coverage made it impossible to ignore the fact that the media called whatever was going on out there a gangland war. Many people were dying. The time I walked by the room late at night and saw them all toasting with brandy, I thought it was probably because they'd just succeeded in some dangerous or clever maneuver.

My father-in-law and my husband had tremendous wills and constantly practiced self-discipline. They were always on guard and vigilant. Nothing came into the house unless they knew where it came from. They were masters at getting people to do things for them, and seemed to have a knack for reading people's minds while keeping their own true thoughts hidden. I suppose these are leadership qualities. I could see that my father-in-law stood out among men. Whenever he opened his mouth the room fell silent, whether there were thirty men in it or two. Men came by day and night to talk to him.

I was confused. On the one hand I loathed what I knew was going on, while on the other hand Bill and his father acted as though they had a noble mission, as though they were on the side of right and their enemy was on the side of wrong. It seemed that all the things *I* thought were wrong were absolutely okay to Bill. I wondered about myself and my upbringing. Our backgrounds were so similar yet so dissimilar. Bill thought he'd married a girl who had been "educated" for the life he led me into. If I had been "educated," would I understand and support my husband? Wouldn't my life be easier that way?

I heard Bill defend the war to a writer who was coming to the house. His name was Gay Talese and he would write the book called *Honor Thy Father*, which was about my husband. He ate dinner with us sometimes but mostly he stayed in the background jotting down things on his pad, and at times he asked questions. One evening at dinner Bill made an analogy between the Vietnam War and the war he was fighting: Nations go to war over money and territory and power. Soldiers get killed and it's acceptable. Families have wars for much the same reasons, and soldiers get killed.

I listened to this and remembered a story told to me by one of the women at a party we had. I'd told her I worried about my husband being in that element, and she'd said, "What? I'd rather live in an Italian neighborhood than anywhere. You got no crime. I'm from Brooklyn. We don't lock our doors. We don't have to. One night there was a black guy following a young woman down my street. A man in a car just watched. Soon other men were watching this guy following the girl up the stairs to her building. When she opened the door he pushed her in. In about three seconds the men were on him. They grabbed that guy and threw him off the roof. On my street there were always eyes that watch." Another woman told me another story. Her family had fallen on hard times and the baker was asked by someone, she never knew who, to make sure they always had bread. I really didn't know what I thought about that. It was good that the men kept the neighborhood safe, but did they have to kill the intruder? I was confused. All I knew for certain was that if the Bonannos were fighting a war, I wished they'd do it somewhere else.

I figured that if Bill was some kind of general, then I was the cook at the command post. And I resented it. If they were at war, I wondered, what in the world were they doing in my house? With my kids. My little kids. Since I didn't know who was who or what was what, and since none of the faces or names were familiar to me except from the recent past, I was afraid that maybe this was a good place for my husband and his father and their men because my family might be part of the enemy, and if I'm part of the enemy then the enemy won't come here. Or maybe they were at my house because my husband was responsible for the lives of his men and his father. They were in the middle of a war and had to keep everything looking normal. I didn't realize at the time, because no one bothered to tell me, that a judge had ordered Mr. Bonanno to live there.

In any case, I resented them for drawing me and my children into it all. At night I locked myself in my closet, fell on my knees, and cried out to the Lord in prayer to make them all go away. I was furious in my heart because I felt Bill owed me a normal life. And although Hank was wonderful and warm and could sometimes make me laugh, and Pete was kind enough to help me clear the table and take out the garbage, I could not look the others in the eye. I tried to ignore them, but they were always there. There is nothing worse than being forced to live in a situation you don't accept.

But worst of all were our children, who were suffering. They came home with stories of how other children had told them their father was a gangster. They got into fights when kids called them "Bananas." They couldn't invite other kids in to play because the house was filled with men. Joseph was as nervous and thin and sickly as ever. Chuck stayed outside a lot, building things like a two-story tree house with wall-to-wall carpeting, and Gigi stuck close to me. Tore, though, was the one who loved the men. He was always fighting and wrestling with them and wishing he could go wherever they went. I worried a little about Tore. He was the most independent of my children. His

first day of nursery school, he just up and left and
walked the five blocks home, crossing three main
streets. He was happiest when he was outside and
had a feeling of no boundaries. And he had a temper like I'd never seen on anyone except his father.
It broke my heart that the kids were subjected to
such a life. But, I suppose, they didn't even know
what "normal" was, so they didn't really miss it.

I formed a plan. I decided to become a den
mother for Chuck's Cub Scout pack. When all
these innocent little kids came to my house once a
week, I thought that surely my father-in-law would
object and maybe leave.

The first day six of them came marching in. Mr.
Bonanno was reading in an easy chair. He looked
up, smiled, then stood, and as courtly as could be,
he said, "Chuck, you brought some friends. Little
soldiers. Come here, children."

They gathered around him and he said,
"Where'd you get those medals? You must be
brave men."

They told him that they were very brave. They
told him what each medal was earned for. He patted them on their shoulders. He laughed deep in his
throat and nodded his head. The kids acted like
adults act when they're around Grandpa Bonanno.
They couldn't take their eyes off the man. Finally
he said, "Well, you boys have a good meeting. I'll
see you later," and left, carrying his thick book to
his room.

After that, my father-in-law made a point of
greeting the boys, fussing over them a little, then

leaving them to go in and out and about their business.

Bill, however, was smiling less and less. He looked as though the weight of the world were on his shoulders. There were often times when he'd leave for a week or two and I would have no money for gas unless I dipped into the stack of twenties I'd hidden away. Asking my father-in-law for money was out of the question; I had too much pride for that. It seemed that even when Bill was home, he was so distracted, he wasn't there. Sometimes when he left he'd be gone for weeks, and then for some reason, rather than coming in the front door of his own house, he'd sneak in in the middle of the night, waking me from a sound sleep to make passionate, almost desperate, love. Other times he sneaked me out of the house in the backseat of a car to make love or blindfolded me so I could not see the motel he took me to.

What was happening to my life? Bill and I had hardly had an opportunity to live alone together with our children since our family became complete, and they were growing up fast.

I was relieved beyond words when, for the Thanksgiving and Christmas after my father-in-law moved in, he got permission from the court to spend the holidays with his family in Tucson. With him went all the men, and Bill and I had a six-week reprieve. I was in heaven. Not only was I alone with my family, but I had my husband home for Christmas. I decorated my home so beautifully, it could have come out of *Family Circle*. Our kids

were all excited about Santa, and Bill came through
with money for toys and a lot of food.

In our families we have a traditional Christmas
celebration. We have a fish feast on Christmas Eve
and another lavish feast on Christmas after we've
awakened and opened our presents. But the most
traditional thing we do is feel thankful for having
each other. Having our family close is something
we never take for granted. This year, my mother
was there and Bill's Aunt Marion and Uncle Jim,
as were some of Bill's cousins and their families.
There was a blizzard on Christmas Eve, and after
midnight we all, even the children, ran out into the
snow and had a snowball fight. We couldn't go to
midnight mass that year but we did have spinge
and sausage. Then everyone slept over. I think if
Bill had his way, everyone would always sleep
over on Christmas Eve. Christmas day dinner was
late and lavish, with lasagna and prime rib and
good Italian pastries. I was truly full and happy.

But after the New Year, 1967, the men returned,
and so did my unhappiness and resentment a hun-
dredfold. It built and built, until finally, in the heat
of July, it reached the breaking point.

One day Bill came home and said, "Make up the
green couch."

That was my living-room couch and nobody had
slept on it yet. I was not about to give up my living
room to the men too. I didn't say a word. I was
learning to fight. You don't threaten by saying,
"I'm leaving." You just leave.

My stack of twenties had been reduced to $360.

I took it all, packed the four kids and some clothes into the car, and left without Bill's knowledge. We stayed in a motel one night, and then I found an inexpensive apartment in Long Beach near the shore. It was a basement with no linens or kitchenware, but it was paradise to me. We played on the beach. We played in the park. I bought TV dinners, then reused the aluminum plates to cook with. I bought bread and milk. No cookies. No cereal. If the kids wanted to pick on something I gave them bread. It was the cheapest way to go, and they never complained.

Some boys had moved into the apartment upstairs and I watched them come and go. They wore shorts and T-shirts and drank beer on their porch. They became friends with the kids then began flirting with me, saying, "Hi, Rosalie," and inviting me up for a beer, which I always refused. The truth was they frightened me. I didn't know what to make of them. They seemed so young, so carefree, yet we were practically the same age. I wished I had the courage just to talk to them. I hated myself for having no guts.

We were in our little apartment for three weeks when it began to rain and didn't let up for another week. The basement, which was damp to begin with, became sodden. Gigi developed a cough and Joseph's asthma began to verge on dangerous. He was coughing through the night and spitting up a lot of phlegm. I was down to my last twenty dollars, so I called Bill. At first he wouldn't talk to me. I talked to Hank, who told me the locks on all

the doors had been changed and I couldn't go
home. I was afraid to go to my family for fear of
what Bill might do, what kind of scene he would
make. I pleaded with Hank. I told him to tell Bill
the kids were sick. I had no money. I had to talk
to him. Finally Bill got on the phone and agreed to
come to Long Beach.

When he arrived, he showed no anger. He was
cold and remote, as though he were conducting a
business deal. He told me to stay in a motel where
he'd already made a reservation. He gave me
money to bring Joseph to the doctor. We lived at
that motel for a week, which the kids enjoyed because there was a pool and a TV but which made
me awfully nervous. I'd never thought it possible
that he wouldn't take me back until then.

I wondered if Bill didn't let me come home right
away because he had lost face in front of his father
and now he had to explain that he was letting me
come back. In any case, after that week, I went
home with a feeling of panic in my stomach. What
if I were to be punished? What if Mr. Bonanno
would not speak to me? Bill was hardly speaking
to me. What if all the men gave me the cold shoulder?

Bill pulled into the driveway, and when I got
out, he pulled back out. Mr. Bonanno was talking
to Pete in the living room when I walked in. He
smiled when he saw me, said hello to me and the
children, then went back to his talk. Hank was leaning against the counter in the kitchen. When I
walked in, he said, "Nice day, huh?"

"Yes," I said. It was cooler and sunny.

I could see that there were no crumbs on the counters or dirty dishes anywhere, but the floor badly needed a mopping.

"Hey, Tore," Hank said. "Bet you don't know how to fight."

"No, sir," Tore said. He always took the bait.

"Oh, yeah? Well, put up your dukes and prove it."

Tore put his fists up near his face and bounced on his knees.

"Come on," I said. "You boys bring your bags into your room and wash your hands. It's almost time for lunch."

Hank dropped the game and Tore took a jab at his knees.

"Hey!" Hank yelled as Tore ran down the hall and pushed Joseph out of his way as he shot past.

Since it was nearly noon, I set Gigi up with some crayons and paper at the kitchen table, then opened five cans of tuna for sandwiches.

And so life returned to normal. No one ever mentioned my leaving or acted like I'd been gone, which made me feel more than a little strange. Then I found out that it had been my brother-in-law who had come to stay on the green couch. The grand jury was subpoenaing people right and left, and whenever they subpoenaed someone from out of town, like Bill's sister's husband, Greg, we usually put them up. I would have liked nothing better than to have seen Greg. If Bill had only said, "Make up the couch for Greg," everything would have been different. But, as usual, Bill believed I should just do what he said, ask no questions, and trust that it was for the best.

And I suppose, as usual, I'd expected him to read my mind. I'd never complained about feeling neglected or put upon. I'd never voiced my fears that he was hiding behind my skirts. I never told him I wished he'd move his command post somewhere else. So Bill had been genuinely surprised when I left.

The war seemed to be taking more and more of a toll. It was in the papers constantly. Money was more scarce than ever. Then, in February, Bill had to leave New York to defend himself in Arizona against a claim that he owed back taxes for 1959–1961. To finance his trip, he was given a credit card that belonged to a man named Don Torrillo. I recognized the name. He owned the house we lived in.

A few days after Bill left, Hank's wife came over for a visit. She was very upset. She told me Hank had said that the war was ending and that the Bonannos were thinking about pulling out of New York. She said that Bill had invited Hank to go along on the trip and that Hank wanted to move out West with Bill. Frances said she'd told Hank no. Absolutely not. She didn't want to go. She figured that maybe if Bill were gone Hank would go back to being normal, get a regular job again. Besides, her father was in the hospital and she was loath to leave her house, which was her only security.

Bill was still away on March 8, which was Gigi's fourth birthday, when Hank got shot coming out of the warehouse. The children saw his picture in the newspaper. His head was bleeding in the gutter. I have no memory of actually saying this, but the children remember that when they pointed at the picture and asked me what had happened to Uncle Hank, I said, "He fell off the curb and hit his head."

Bill never made it back for the funeral. Frances sat bravely next to her son and across from her husband's body at the wake. I'd prayed for Hank and would pray more. I told Frances this and handed her a card in which I'd put fifty dollars that I'd taken from my squirreled-away money. She didn't open the envelope as I stood there. I wished it could have been more. I knew how alone Frances must have felt. I knew how I would feel if I were Frances. I often wondered if maybe Hank would still be alive if he had gone with Bill.

Bill never explained to me why Hank's family wasn't taken care of, but he has explained in a more general way what happens in his world when someone gets in trouble: If you work for a company and the company tells you to go to Phoenix for a couple of days to put a deal together, and you go to Phoenix and do your job but in the process of doing your job you get into trouble, the employer has an obligation to help you. But if you decide to stay a couple of days longer, the company is not obliged or expected to pay your expenses for those extra couple of days. Or if, say, the employee

goes out and finds a guy in bed with his wife and
shoots the guy, then that has nothing to do with the
employer either and the employer is not obligated
to help him.

Although my husband has never told me this directly, I think maybe Hank was taking his life into
his own hands by staying behind. Whatever the reason was that Hank died, Frances was left to fend
for herself and her family, and it broke my heart.
I felt terrible for Fran and her children.

After many sleepless nights I tried my best to
put Hank and what had happened out of my mind,
but still I was scared to death. It had brought death
home, so to speak, and I was terrified for my husband, my children, and myself.

CHAPTER 11

BILL came home soon afterward. He didn't mention Hank and neither did I.

Now I turned inward and said this poem by Tolstoy for comfort:

> CHRIST teaches men
> that there is something in them
> which lifts them above this life,
> with its hurries, its pleasures, its
>   sorrows
> and fears, hurts and disappointments.
> He who understands Christ's teachings
> feels like a bird that did
> not know it has wings
> and now suddenly realizes
> that it can fly,
> can be free,
> and no longer needs to fear.

It had been more than a year now since I picked up a paper, because it was too painful to see the Bonanno name linked with death and violence. Now a headline jumped out at me as I stood at a deli counter waiting for some cold cuts. REPORT JOE

BANANAS AND SON MARKED FOR RUBOUT. Bill had come home that same evening. I examined his face for signs of fear or worry. I wanted to see if he looked like a man marked for a rubout. I couldn't tell. Other than tired from his journey, he seemed the same as always. A little edgy, but he'd been that way for years now. I concluded there was nothing unusual.

Until the next morning, when I sat up in bed to start the day and felt him reach up and rest his hand on the center of my back, then begin to rub it. "Ro," he said, "we're moving. We're going to California."

I had been asking Bill to move us to California for months now. My sister Annie lived there with her family, my sister Vickie was going to Berkeley, and Bill's sister Catherine lived in the same area as my sisters. My mother had been threatening to move too. In California I'd have baby-sitters. My children would be raised with their cousins. We could have family gatherings. Surely there would be no war in California. There would be the possibility for a different life. But Bill had never responded. He'd seemed not only impervious to my California sell job but utterly uninterested. Now I turned in the bed and looked at him. He wasn't smiling. This was no joke. He was dead serious. I pinned him down by the shoulders and bounced him on the bed. "You're not kidding? We're moving? I can't believe it. I'm so happy."

"Better get ready."

"How long do I have? When are we leaving?"

"This morning."

My joy instantly turned to panic. "That's impossible."

"No, it isn't. Just dress the kids and we'll go."

"Bill, what about the furniture?"

"We'll send for it."

"Clothes?"

"All right. So pack some clothes. Jesus. You've been crying about moving to California, now I tell you we're going and all you see is the trouble."

I think a major requirement of my marriage has been to be able to roll with the punches. I have never been very good at it. But this time I tried like crazy. I packed a couple of suitcases and told the kids each to bring a pillow and a blanket. We left at dawn with an escort in front of our car and one behind. We were leaving New York when all of a sudden the kids opened the windows and started to sing "California here we come . . . !"

During our journey news of Martin Luther King's assassination came over the radio. Bill said, "You see? He was getting too powerful and the government had to cut him down."

"There's always such a fine line between life and death," I said. "You must always be ready."

"Ready for what?" Joseph asked.

"To face God. Because he's going to judge you."

Bill was silent, but I knew he'd heard me.

It was April, and California was verdant and bursting with flowers. The sun shone every day. The warm air felt comforting. All I could think was that

I never wanted to leave here and why didn't we move sooner? We stayed at Bill's sister's house for a couple of weeks while Bill and I went looking for apartments. We found out pretty quickly that if we admitted to having four children, the landlord's face changed from friendliness to indifference, and although none of them actually said, "Sorry, you've got too many kids," neither did they offer us a lease. So, when we found an apartment, which was in a row of rather shabby two-family houses, had two bedrooms and was furnished, we told the landlord we had two children and signed a lease. Things were looking up. It may not have been the best house in the world, but Bill and I had actually looked for it and chosen it together. In a short time we were settled.

Bill assumed I respected him for standing up for what he believed in. But I was only happy that we were far away from that New York scene, from all those men and all those meetings in our house. Here in California there would be no more drawn curtains or the occasional car crawling past or person walking by, staring at our house, curious to see a mobster or a mobster's wife. Perhaps the Bonanno name wasn't notorious enough to have made it into the California papers. Perhaps we would have anonymity here. If the Bonannos had left New York, maybe as a force they were defunct. Maybe Bill would have no choice but to get a job.

This hope lasted about half a second. We had just moved into the apartment when Bill took a trip to see his father in Tucson and didn't return for several weeks. In fact, in the months to come he was home only for a few days at a time. I did not know what he was doing or where he was going at first. But once the summer rolled around I knew and so did the rest of the nation. He was in Tucson guarding the Bonanno house because it had been bombed.

Surely this meant they really were marked for execution. Had he and his father been followed from New York? Was it possible to escape being killed once those people had made up their minds?

I didn't want to know. I wanted my husband to be safe. I wanted his father and mother to be safe. I wanted me and my children to be safe. I needed desperately for things to be just ordinary. I would not think about what my husband was facing in Tucson. I would pray every night for his family's safety, but I would picture or imagine nothing. I would make what I had control over, the day-to-day with my children, as predictable and orderly and routine as possible.

As soon as we'd moved in, I'd entered Chuck, who was in the fourth grade, and Joseph, who was in the second, in the school at the end of the street, then developed a daily routine. After I packed their lunches and sent them off, I dressed the two younger ones and sent them out to play in the yard. Then I got to work in earnest. I did the breakfast dishes and scoured the sink and wiped down the counters and all the appliances. Then I mopped the kitchen floor, which I waxed every Saturday, then did the front steps. Next I wiped down the walls in the hallway, because no matter how many times you tell kids not to put their hands on the walls, they never hear you. After that was done I made my way upstairs to the bathroom and bedrooms. By the time lunch was over, I started baking a dessert and making other dinner preparations. Sometimes Annie and her husband, Louie, and their two children ate over; sometimes we ate at their house. But whether or not we ate together, Annie and I saw each other just about every day.

Really, the only thing that bothered me besides the usual "I wish I had a normal husband" blues, or at least a physically present one, was my kitchen floor. The linoleum was torn and buckling in places. This made me feel as though I was living in some kind of tenement while I was intent on viewing our life in California as an improvement. So, at great risk, I arranged for the landlord to come and take a look at it. If he came to my house and discovered four kids instead of two he might throw us out. I didn't know exactly when he would drop by, so I couldn't hide the extra kids at Annie's. I tried my best to prepare them. I sat them at the dinner table and said, "Now, listen carefully. It's a sin to lie, but Mommy had no choice. I told the landlord I only had two children so we could get this apartment."

"Why?" said Joseph, who was seven.

"Because landlords want you to have only a few children because children sometimes make a mess and wreck things."

"We don't," said Joseph.

"Chuck does," said Tore, five years old.

"What do you mean?" I asked him.

"He dug a hole in the yard."

"You dug a hole, Chuck?"

"Yes." Chuck was ten.

"What for?"

"I needed to make some mud. You weren't supposed to tell." He glared at Tore.

"That's right, Tore," I said, trying to take the role of his father by being adamant on the point of snitching. "But Chuckie, what did you need mud for?"

"To make a mud hut."

Chuck always had to be building something to be happy.

"You need a lot of mud, though, Ma."

"I don't think you should build a hut, Chuck. Maybe we could see about getting you some lumber."

"Oh, boy!"

"I like mud," said four-year-old Gigi.

"I know you do. But you have to listen carefully now."

"I threw rocks in the hole," said Tore.

"You're not supposed to throw rocks," said Joseph. "Daddy said."

I wished Daddy were here this minute. Why was it that as soon as he opened his mouth everybody listened and as soon as I opened mine everybody else did too?

"Quiet!" I said.

"Shhhh," one started, then they all chimed in.

I closed my eyes until they stopped. "The landlord is going to drop by one day, and when he does Tore and Gigi have to hide upstairs, and we have to pretend that Chuckie and Joe are my only kids."

"That's not fair!" Tore said, getting red in the face.

"Shhh," Chuck said.

"I know it's not fair, Tore, but it's not for real. It's because I can only have two children and Chuckie and Joe are the oldest."

I don't know how I did it, but Tore finally agreed.

The landlord showed up on a Saturday. Tore had been mad at me during lunch because he'd wanted bologna and I'd given him peanut butter and jelly, or the other way around, so when I saw the landlord's truck pull into the drive and told Tore and Gigi, "Quick. Run up the stairs," Tore did it but reluctantly. The landlord hadn't been in the kitchen for a minute, though, before Tore ran back down the stairs, stuck one foot forward, and said, "My mother has four kids. I'm Tore. Gigi's upstairs and that's Joe and that's Chuck."

The landlord burst out laughing. "That's all right, lady," he said. "Anybody who swabs the front steps every day can have ten kids as far as I'm concerned."

I wasn't even mad. I figured if Tore, my wildest, could snitch on his mother, there was no way he'd fit into my husband's world.

• • •

Aside from being basically husbandless, and troubled with Joseph's asthma, which seemed to be getting worse and at times had been so bad that we'd had to bring him to the emergency room for medications that would allow him to breathe, life in California was pretty good. Bill had arranged for me to have my brother-in-law Louie's car, and sometimes I took the kids for drives on the immaculate California roads. They were wider here than back East and as smooth as glass. The surroundings were beautifully landscaped. This was at the very beginning of the boom in technology in San Jose and there was a lot of construction going on. Everything seemed so new and wide open and possible here.

I began to think that maybe a way to allay my fears would be to have a career and become financially independent. The first thing would be to find some training. I'd received in the mail an aptitude test for computer training. I took it, scored high, and then a woman came by my house one evening and sold me on a course in computer programming. She said that it was the career of the future, that since there were so many companies starting up and so few trained people to fill the ever-increasing positions, I would have my choice of jobs. For one thousand dollars I could complete the course work that would qualify me to be a computer program-

mer. Since Bill was gone so much now, I figured
I could take a class.

In the fall, when Tore started half-days in kindergarten and went off in the morning with his
older brothers, I took the pile of fives and tens and
twenties I'd hoarded and invested it in a programming course at the computer school. I was able to
arrange my classes so that I was gone from home
while the two older ones were in school. Annie was
my savior by picking up Tore after kindergarten
and bringing him along with Gigi to her house.

I did not tell Bill. Aside from asking about his
children, my husband asked few questions about
what was going on in San Jose. He was having big
problems. The bombings in Tucson had stopped by
now. They'd been part of a plot by a member of
the FBI who tried to ignite new animosities between the warring factions of my husband's world.
But serious difficulties were brewing in New York.
When Bill used Don Torrillo's credit card in Arizona, and a shopkeeper put a call in to the credit-
card company to check the credit limit, Bill was
unable to answer personal questions about Don
Torrillo, so the shopkeeper kept the credit card and
reported Bill to the authorities. Torrillo said he'd
been bullied by Hank into giving up his card, and
now Bill was charged with fifty counts of mail
fraud. If convicted on all counts, he could serve
220 years in prison.

Bill had to travel back and forth to New York
to consult with lawyers and to work on his own
defense. How he got the money for the flights, or

for the suits he wore, or for the lawyers, I have no idea. I had to keep changing Joseph's doctors because we couldn't meet their bills, and more than once our rent was overdue. This made me very nervous, so to escape thinking about our money plight, I concentrated more intently on computer school.

I was the only woman in a class of thirty. In those days it wasn't enough to learn computer language; you also had to wire the program. To say I had no mechanical aptitude is an understatement. But my logic was good and so was my need to make something of myself. I enjoyed being engaged in something. And I enjoyed the friendship I'd developed with a young man around twenty-five. His name was Tim and he was the brain of the class. From the first meeting at our first class, he'd taken me under his wing. We were partners when we ran our programs. Soon he was driving me to class too. This was an entirely new experience for me. I'd never had a friendship with a man before. Although I didn't talk about myself much, I did tell him about my children, and he told me about his mother and father and siblings, and we both sang the praises of California and shared our dreams of a future of high-paying jobs.

For a long time, by a stroke of luck, Bill wasn't home on the days Tim picked me up. But, inevitably, one day he was.

It was a Wednesday, and for some reason he'd come home from New York the day before and was making no signs of leaving. Naturally, I got nervous.

Back in September, when I'd told him I'd enrolled in computer school, he'd wiped his mouth with his napkin and asked me for more ice water. I filled a fresh pitcher, poured him a glass, and watched his face for some reaction. There was none. I didn't trust it. I knew my husband well enough to know that he'd been trained as a diplomat by his father, and one of the staples of the diplomat's art is never to let the other guy know what you're thinking. The next day he said, "So, where'd you get the money?"

I said I'd saved it.

"You saved it," he said, not believing. "Your brother give it to you?"

"No."

"Your mother?" She'd recently moved to California.

"No."

"Don't give me that," he said. "Somebody had to give it to you. You got it from your mother behind my back."

I remained silent. It must have hurt Bill's pride that I would ever have to ask my family for anything. He was the man and he should do the providing.

But he never mentioned or objected to my schooling and this was a little shocking. It's true that Bill had had no objection to my going to college back in Flagstaff, but we had no children then. For a first-generation Sicilian-American (especially one in my husband's world) to allow his wife to go to school and leave his children was a very progressive act, bordering on heresy. I know this was difficult for Bill and it took a certain amount of subduing of his pride, but I think he knew this meant a lot to me. He could see I was happier now, not living under such a dark cloud. Also, I think he had faced the fact that he might go to jail and that I would have to support myself and our children if he did.

Now, with him home and Tim due any second to pick me up, I was actually sweating. I'm sure he noticed. He was sitting in his chair in the living room, a book on his lap, but he kept glancing up from it, at me standing by the window, holding my books to my chest, feeling my heart beat against them. When I saw Tim's car round the bend, I said, "Well, I'm going," and walked out the door, aware with every step I took that Bill was at the window watching. When I slammed the door and Tim pulled away, I slumped down on the seat from relief. I'd been afraid Bill would yell for me to come back, or, worse, come running out and pull Tim from the car, maybe slug him, but he'd done neither. Nor did he ever so much as mention my young man friend, except many years later, when I overheard him telling a friend the shock he'd felt at witnessing his wife walk out of his house, books clutched to her chest, and enter the car of a strange man. He realized this was the beginning of a new way of life. He said he had never imagined a thing like that could happen in his life. Then he said, "But you know something, part of me was proud."

No doubt about it. It was the sixties and the world was changing.

So was my life. In November 1968 Bill's court case began, and it did not look good. When he came home on the weekends, having traveled between New York and Tucson and then back to California, we began to entertain the possibility that he might go away to jail, and this time it would be for much longer than three months, maybe ten years. After I'd finished my computer course, I'd been informed that to get a programmer's job I'd first need a college degree. I had no idea what I would live on if Bill went to jail. I began to badger him about getting me a house. "Set me up, set me up," was my constant refrain.

One of my favorite pastimes since we'd moved to San Jose was to ride around with my kids for entire days searching for a house. There was something about living in an apartment that rubbed me the wrong way. It was not healthy for the kids. I had already been called to school because Joe and Chuck had been caught with pictures from *Playboy* magazine. Evidently, someone had discarded the magazines in the alley, and the boys had found them and taken them to school. I was appalled and embarrassed that my children had done this. When we got home I gave them the lecture they heard many times after that.

"You are not ordinary children; you have to try twice as hard to be good, you have to be better than everybody else. The world won't give you a second chance because of your name."

Finally, one Sunday, which I've always thought of as family day, Bill was sitting in the living room after our large dinner, which it was traditional to serve at three o'clock, and I said, "Sundays will be the saddest if you go to jail."

"I'm trying my damnedest, Rosalie."

"I know. I'm just afraid. I wish I could feel more secure. If I had my own house . . ."

I braced myself because it was not unusual for me to invoke a rage in my husband by mentioning the words "my own house." But this time he closed his eyes and pinched the bridge of his nose. "Go ahead," he said. "Go find one."

I was in the car the first thing the next morning. The boys were in school and Gigi stood next to me, her hand wrapped around my neck. I was looking for what I'd been calling "my dream house." I'd already found it a couple of months after we'd moved to San Jose. It had been under construction then and I couldn't remember exactly where I'd seen it. All I remembered was that it was a distance from where we lived and nearer to Annie. It was on a cul de sac, which would be perfect for the children. Gigi and I must have driven around looking for that house for four hours. Finally, I gave up, had lunch at Annie's, then went to a realtor Annie knew. The realtor performed a miracle and found me the house. It was in Campbell, a suburb of San Jose. And another miracle happened. The house had been lived in for only one year, but was now for sale. This was no coincidence. This house had been meant for me from the minute I'd peeked at it through its new windows.

It was perfect. The living room and dining rooms were all one, which would allow me to open up the table when we entertained a lot of people. Bill would like that. The kitchen counters were tile and had a splash back, which I'd always wanted. And there were four bedrooms with four closets, a place for everyone and everything. There was a gorgeous stone fireplace with an exposed stone chimney in the living room and a beautiful beamed ceiling. By this time my taste had changed and I appreciated the natural look indoors.

The washer and dryer were on the same floor as everything else, so I wouldn't have to be marching up and down the stairs of the basement every time I threw a load in. The only drawback I could see was the backyard, which even after two years was still a sea of mud.

I rushed home and excitedly told Bill about the house. He nodded his head and said, "Good." He was distracted, as he seemed to be most of the time now. He was often in New York, and when he was home he pored over law books. I had always known my husband was an intelligent man, but my respect for him grew when I picked up one of those books one day and tried to read it. It might as well have been in Latin. And when the details of how we got our house came to my knowledge, I had to admire Bill for his resourcefulness.

It was not possible for us to own a house, because if we had any assets the IRS would seize them. Bill knew that his uncle Jim had a soft spot in his heart for California, but Uncle Jim's wife, Aunt Marion, couldn't seem to tear herself away from her sisters in Brooklyn. Aunt Marion was childless and loved Bill like her own son. Bill sent Aunt Marion cards on Mother's Day and called her every holiday. He made a big fuss over her birthdays, sending her flowers when he couldn't be there. Now he approached her and Uncle Jim with a proposition. If they would put a down payment on a house and allow us to live there, we would make the mortgage payments. Uncle Jim was sick, but when he was well they could move to California and have their own house waiting.

Aunt Marion agreed, and we moved into the little cul de sac in Campbell, opened up our dining table and had a feast for twenty. The housewarming coincided with a visit from Bill's father, so our families were together to celebrate. I finally had what I'd been hoping for my whole life, a house I'd chosen myself, my family with me. My joy should've been complete. A stranger at that gathering would never have guessed that we were warding off so much trouble. Inevitably, as trouble will, it came to pass.

In March 1970, I received a phone call from Bill. He said, "Well, Ro, I've got some bad news." He'd been convicted of all charges and sentenced to four years in prison. "Look at it this way, babe, I'll only be little over forty when I get out. We'll have our whole lives ahead of us."

I began to tremble uncontrollably with the effort

of holding back tears. I did not want to crumble and burden him with my sadness when it was he who had to spend four years of his life in jail. I could think of nothing to say. What came out was, "You'll still be handsome."

I'd imagined he'd come home, pack a bag, and go off to jail, but that's not how it works. Bill had appeals pending, and no one knew when the court would finally tell him to report to prison. Meanwhile, we decided to make the best of our lives while we waited. Bill wanted to treat his kids to a time they'd never forget. He rented a forty-foot houseboat and invited my sister Annie and his sister Catherine and their five kids along with our four. With his brother Joe there were fourteen of us on a boat sailing through the channels of the Sacramento River, and the San Joaquin delta sloughs.

Bill was the captain. I was the navigator. The only problem was that Bill had never captained a boat in his life and I found marks on the map but no buoys in the water. More than once we anchored the boat in the evening and in the morning were grounded—we didn't realize this river had tides. One time I started saying an act of contrition because I was sure we were done for. Bill spotted a huge ship coming toward us, being pulled by two tugboats, trailing four-feet-high swells. He thought the best maneuver would be to cut right through them. "Hold on," he yelled as we rode the top of the wave. When we dived down it, the next wave ran right over us. A torrent of water took everything that wasn't tied down with it: pots, pans, dishes, spaghetti, everything. I panicked, jumped down below, and began to throw life jackets on deck. But by then we'd run through the swells and everyone laughed at me like I was a crazy woman. "What? You going for a swim?" Bill said.

It was in the spirit of that trip that nobody was the least bit disturbed that half of all our belongings were floating around us in the water.

By the fall, however, we were all feeling the strain of Bill's leaving. We'd had several false-alarm going-away parties, and we were edgy and exhausted from having felt all those strong emotions only to find that Bill's departure had been delayed another time. I started painting again. And many of those oils are hanging to this day in my friends' homes.

We were having dinner a week before Christmas with Mom and Dad Bonanno at our *compare* Jimmy's house when the phone rang.

"It's Al Krieger, Bill," said Jimmy.

We had been expecting the call for days. When Bill returned to the table, the morbid look on his face told us that the definite time had come.

"Quanno?" ("when" in Italian) said Mr. Bonanno.

"January eighteenth."

We could not finish dinner.

The news was horribly decisive but in a way it relieved us. We knew where we stood.

On the morning he was to leave we all had breakfast. Bill had prepared the children over the months, telling them that he'd be going away to jail for a couple of years. Now he said, "Well, kids, Dad's leaving today for jail. I won't be living here in the house for a while, but you can come and visit." Gigi began to cry. Bill lifted her to his lap and stroked her head as he spoke. "Now, I want you kids to write me and I'll write you back. Chuck?"

"Yes?"

"You're the oldest, so you make sure you take care of your mother."

"Yes, sir." He nodded his head gravely.

"Joseph, I want you to try to eat better and get yourself strong."

Joseph nodded.

"Tore, I don't want you picking on your sister. I want you to listen to your mother and practice your football, okay?"

"Is Chuck the boss of me now?"

"He's your older brother."

"He's not my father."

"No. He's not your father."

I took deep long breaths. I did not want to cry. Why is it that only when you're about to lose something do you realize how much you value it? Why had I been so hard on Bill? Why had I harped on him and nagged at him and criticized his character? The poor man was facing four years away from his family, four years of prison life. I wanted to hold him. I wanted to hang on and not let him out of my sight. His fingers as he stroked his daughter's hair seemed so long and graceful, delicate almost. "Bill," I said, "let me go to Los Angeles." He'd be interned at Terminal Island there, and we'd already discussed how he wanted to leave the house alone.

"No, Ro."

"Then at least to the airport. Let me ride in the car to the airport. Please."

"I can't do that. It's better this way. I just can't."

When I saw him place Gigi back on her feet and stand up from the table and walk to the door, I lost control. I ran after him. I hugged him hard. I hung on to his neck, weeping. I wasn't thinking about my children now. I wasn't thinking about anything. I was just feeling grief. The children began to cry behind me. Bill gently removed my hands from his neck. He cupped my face in his hands, kissed me, and left.

CHAPTER 12

As I stood on a long line at the Santa Clara welfare office, looking at all the babies, crowded by men in beards and rags and women with wild hair who smelled funny—I'd later learn it was of incense and musk—I couldn't help but think of my wedding. I pictured myself as a little princess standing at the top of the aisle in her fairy-tale gown and I remembered how I'd felt not the slightest bit of guilt for its extravagant cost, as though it had been my divine right to have the most beautiful gown I could imagine. How far away from all that I had come.

Before Bill left he'd instructed me to apply for welfare. He reasoned that since the government had made it impossible for him to have savings or to show income, and since it had confiscated his assets and now had taken him out of commission, the government could damn well support his family while he did time in jail. I, however, no matter what my husband's logic, felt a deep sense of shame to ask the United States of America to support me and my children.

I couldn't stop thinking about our wedding money either. Pouches and pouches of it dumped into a suitcase. What had happened to that? Probably the same thing that had happened to my magnificent five-carat diamond. It had disappeared in the hands of my husband. Around the same time as the credit-card trouble began, Bill told me he wanted to pawn my ring. He said, "Look, Ro, I'm not going to use it to go to Vegas or New York or the Caribbean. It's for Wally (his cousin). He's starting an ad agency and he needs the money. I told him only for a couple of months. We'll get it back. I know how much this ring means to you."

Two years later Bill and I were driving in the car when he said "Rosalie" in a certain way that made me know I was in for bad news. "I'm sorry. But you should know this. Your ring? You're not getting it back. I'm heartsick about it, Ro. If I knew this would happen I never would've loaned it."

I turned my face away and looked at the well-groomed lawns zooming past.

"I did what I could. I went to the pawnbroker. I know him. He said, 'I already told Wally. I'm just one of the partners here. I got three other partners. They wanted the money or they wanted to get rid of the ring.'

"What was I going to do? Shoot him in the head? We're talking money. I turned the town upside down, Ro. For two years I looked for the ring. I can't find it."

I still couldn't look at him.

He reached over and put his hand on my knee. I let it stay there.

· · ·

When I was finally ushered to a desk, I filled out some forms while pains shot through my stomach with every question I answered. I was dead sure the woman welfare worker sitting across from me was about to look at me with pity any second and say, "Of course, you realize we'll have to take your house." I know now there was no rational reason for this. We did not own our house. Aunt Marion and Uncle Jim did. So they couldn't confiscate it in return for public assistance, which they probably wouldn't have done even if I did own it. I think it was simply my deepest fear.

The interview turned out to be painless and short. The woman told me to expect a visit from a social worker within the next few weeks, and then, to my astonishment, she handed me a packet of food stamps.

I planned to go straight to the store on my way home, but when I tried to start the car it wouldn't turn over. That was it. I couldn't help it. I rested my forehead on the wheel. I hated Bill at that moment. Before he'd left there'd been so much partying and false merriment, the memory of it sickened my stomach. He'd had plenty of money for fun and for restaurants and lawyers and first-class tickets when he had to fly to New York City, but after I'd begged him to make provisions for me, all he'd come up with was the address of the welfare bureau and our brother-in-law Greg's failing car.

When I tried the car again it started, but on my way home I controlled myself from wailing with indignation, fear, grief, and an abundance of self-pity. Here I was, thirty-five years old, a husband seven hundred miles away, in jail. No job. No skills. A $250 mortgage payment and only about $350 a month expected from welfare. I had five stomachs to feed, ten feet to buy shoes for, and five heads of hair to keep groomed. If anything went wrong with the children, everyone in the world would blame me, including myself.

How could Bill have been so stupid? How could he have risked so much by using someone else's credit cards. Why didn't he worry that the man could turn around and accuse him of stealing it? He knew the authorities were trying to get him on anything they could.

I was devastated when I stepped out of the car and into my house. I took an apple from the refrigerator and cut it into four pieces to try to force myself to eat something. Usually apples made me feel healthy and optimistic, but this time when I took a bite the fruit felt mealy on my tongue and I wanted to spit it out, but I forced myself to swallow. I had to change this whole situation. I'd start by getting a job. I could go to work when the kids were in school. Gigi was in the first grade now, Tore in second, Joseph in fourth, and Chuck in sixth. They went to the same school, right in the neighborhood. But what if Joseph got sick? His asthma attacks had increased. We had endless sleepless nights now when I stroked his head and watched him wheeze. There was nothing I could do to stop it. A few times I'd had to bring him to the emergency room. It scared me to death. They pumped him full of medication there. Sometimes it made him worse. I was lucky if Joseph kept four meals a week down.

I had to stop this crying, this thinking, before the children came home. It only upset them, and the last thing Joseph needed was to feel more frightened. I got a tissue from the kitchen counter, which made me think of Bill again. I wondered if Bill had made provisions for Erica and her children when he'd left her to join me back East.

Bill had never loved me enough. I should face facts.

I collapsed on the couch. Too soon, I heard the door slam. It was Gigi. "Oh, Mom," she said, throwing herself on top of me.

"Baby. Mom's okay. Just a little sad."

"Me too. I wish Daddy weren't in jail. He'd make Tore stop."

"Poor Gigi."

"He's always hitting me and pulling my hair. I hate him."

"Don't say that."

"Daddy would make him stop."

Next Joseph walked in with a fine layer of perspiration on his brow. "Oh, no. Come here," I said, sitting up and swabbing his brow with my tissue.

"Don't," he said, pushing my arm away.

"Mom," Gigi said, pulling at my sleeve.

"Move out of the way." Joseph pushed Gigi and tried to wedge himself between us.

"STOP IT!" I screamed. They stopped cold and stared at me. "Where's Tore?" I said.

"I don't know," said Joseph.

"Tore's playing football in the field," said Gigi.

"With his school clothes? Like I have all the money in the world to replace them?"

"He doesn't care," Joseph said. "And you won't punish him. You'll just yell and he won't listen."

Joseph was right.

"Where's Chuck?"

"I don't know. But I'm watching my shows. I was here first. He can't turn the channel."

It seemed there was never a noncontentious moment with my children since Bill left. Had they always been like this and I hadn't noticed?

When Tore finally showed up after I called him in for dinner, he was covered with dirt. I told him that if he played in his school clothes again he'd be grounded. He smirked, turned to Chuck, and made like he was laughing behind his hand. I ignored it and told him we would wait for him to wash but to make it quick because our dinner was getting cold. When he returned I asked my children how they'd feel if I got a job. "Fine," they said.

"But if I'm working that means I won't have so much time to cook and clean and I'll need your help."

They seemed to agree to this.

"And you can't fight when I'm gone, either."

"Tell Tore," Gigi said.

"Tore?" I said.

"Baby. Baby. Baby," Tore taunted.

"TORE!"

"I want my daddy," Gigi started to cry.

"You're not the only one, stupid girl." Tore stuffed his mouth with mashed potatoes and squirted a dribble down his chin.

"When are we going to visit?" Joe was getting shaky.

"I could read the map," Chuck said.

"I don't know," I said, getting near tears again myself. "The car gave me trouble today."

"I could fix it," Chuck said.

"No, honey, I don't think you can." Chuck had already fixed a leak in the bathroom and had built beautiful floor-to-ceiling shelves in the living room when we moved in a year ago, but he was only eleven and certainly a car was too complicated a machine.

"But how can you get a job if our car breaks down?" he asked.

That did it. I was off and weeping.

"Don't cry," Chuck said. But as soon as dinner was over, the kids went outside and I could hear them laughing and yelling and playing some game on the driveway as I watched my hands go in and out of the sudsy water and my tears burn through the bubbles.

By the time Christine, the social worker, came for her visit at the end of the next week, I was able to restrain myself a little better, at least so that I didn't cry in her presence. I'd been afraid she might be haughty or snobbish, because to have a job like hers she must have been well educated, but I was wrong. She had a head of fiery-red hair and was a rather large woman, although she hid the contours of her body beneath a shapeless sack of a dress. She wore sandals and a clunky, jangly necklace, and was loud and warm and laughed from deep inside her belly. She brought a sack of fruit, which we dumped into a bowl in the middle of the table.

Christine took out a pad and pencil and jotted down our financial and emotional needs. The children, she could see for herself, were out of control. They were running wild through the house, screaming and fighting over everything and anything. I screamed too and it made no difference. I was not setting a good example. Whenever any little thing went wrong, like a light bulb blowing, under my breath I would say, "Your damned father!" I think the kids wished I'd been the one sent to jail instead of him. I told Christine I was worried about this.

I was also worried that if I didn't learn to control my children they might grow up to think that borrowing money, using people, and going to jail was okay.

Christine told me I was worrying too much. Kids are resilient, she said. And they're usually fondest of the missing parent. It was natural. They were anxious and confused too. She told me that she could arrange for me to attend a parent-effectiveness-training course. She could also do group and individual counseling with my kids.

There was hope. She told me I shouldn't be ashamed of being on welfare. Many women in my position had done it. Just as in prison Bill had the initials "O.C." on his file jacket, which stood for Organized Crime, the welfare bureau had a category for us too: "Italian Gangsters."

I told Christine I was planning to get a part-time job and she told me she thought it was a good idea, which encouraged me. I got closer to Christine over the months, although I never opened up to her entirely. It was hard for me to trust outsiders.

She was unlike anyone I'd ever known. She'd had eight children and *three* husbands. And she was nice. She was better than nice, she was wonderful. Cheerful, wise, compassionate. For the life of me, I could not understand how a person could be so nice and still be so immoral as to have had three husbands. Christine was smart too, and accustomed to dealing with people like me, because she knew not to ask questions. I didn't tell Christine much really. I was too well counseled in keeping secrets.

I didn't describe to her how I'd lived in East Meadow behind drawn blinds, furious to be forced into a situation that was intolerable to me yet powerless to do anything about it. Nor did I tell her the details of Bill and Erica back in Arizona, but I did tell her he had had a long-standing affair and how it had hurt and disillusioned me.

I'd expected her to tell me to divorce him, but instead she said, "Honey, you're mixing apples with oranges."

"What do you mean?"

"A man," she said, "sees his wife in one way and girlfriends in another. Your husband still loves you. You are the mother of his children and his wife; an affair's something else entirely. A man like Bill will never leave you for another woman. You can't turn your nose up at that."

"But," I insisted, "he committed a mortal sin. He's a bad person and I've had children with him. My religion doesn't allow me to leave him. You have to understand. I never imagined his being with another woman before we married, let alone thought of his doing it after. He broke the sacred trust of marriage!"

"So there you were, trying to live a moral life with someone you considered immoral?" she said.

"Yes."

"Well, if Bill didn't consider it immoral, did it still make it immoral?"

"Yes. No. Yes. In the eyes of God."

I could barely meet Bill's eyes when I went to visit. I felt shame for him. And I was so angry that he'd left me in this impoverished condition. I didn't realize Bill had done the best he could. He'd asked his cousin Nino to come over once a week to check up on us and report back to him. I let Bill know how frightening it was to take the seven-hour trip in a car I didn't trust. He told me I was exaggerating. The car was fine. It was all in my mind. "You set up your own obstacles," he said. "You always have."

We were sitting in a big, noisy, and crowded room. After the kids had climbed all over him for a while, I gave them some change for the vending machines.

After Bill watched them run off, he told me Joseph looked awful, which he did. "What's his doctor say?"

"I take him to the emergency room."

"You have medical care, don't you? Take him to a specialist."

"But specialists are too expensive."

"Rosalie, welfare pays for it," Bill said, his voice filled with exasperation. "Jesus, don't tell me you're even going to be careful with the government's money."

I didn't believe him. He was the one who never saw the need for health or car insurance. What did he know about anything? He was getting three hot meals a day and a place to sleep in. What did he know about my worries. I didn't trust him or his opinions. Would I ever feel anything but anger for this man?

Gay Talese had finished *Honor Thy Father* by this time, and when I told Bill I was going to look for a part-time job, he must have said something to Gay, because Gay called and told me he'd like to pay for me to go to an employment agency, which found me a job as a keypunch operator at a title-insurance company.

With the money I received from that job and welfare, if I was very frugal, I had just enough to pay the mortgage plus my monthly utilities, to buy gas for the car, and to feed my family. I didn't mind so much not having any extra money because it felt like a luxury just to have checks made in my own name and to be able to budget and pay my bills on time. Control was a consoling feeling.

The only drawback with working was that I had to leave Joseph home alone when he was sick, which caused me some anxiety, and even more guilt. When he was home with asthma, I monitored him every hour by calling and listening to him breathe on the phone, but I worried. We'd stripped the rug from his room and I vacuumed every day, but it made no difference. The medication made him throw up more meals than he kept down. He was so skinny his ribs stuck out like an African famine victim. When I looked at Joseph, I saw how I was failing as a mother.

One evening he turned blue. I was loath to take him to the hospital. I was afraid he would die.

An intern gave Joseph a shot that induced an allergic reaction and he ended up in an oxygen tent at death's door. I watched helplessly as specialists surrounded my baby's frail body. I remembered my father under a rubber sheet so many years before, in so much pain but trying to be strong for me even as he was dying. I began to tremble and felt the tears coming but stopped them. Somehow, like my father, I would have to find strength to fight this fear because if I didn't I might lose my child.

I went into the chapel at the hospital and knelt for an hour. I talked to God and prayed. I told God

I knew he had a plan and I shouldn't question it, but I begged him please not to take Joseph. I prayed for courage to help my son. I prayed for understanding and for an ability to forgive so I could stop being so angry at Bill. I prayed to be able to cope better so Joseph wouldn't be so upset and frightened. I prayed that his illness was not my fault. I told God I would try harder. I told God I trusted that in His divine wisdom He would know the right thing to do. Then I sat back and looked at the stained-glass window. It was of the Virgin Mary; she held the baby Jesus in her arms and stood on top of the world. I wept softly and prayed to Mary too. I asked her to help me be a better mother. I knew she understood how I felt and this gave me comfort.

When I went back to Joseph's room, an intern took me aside and suggested I call a pediatric allergy specialist named Dr. Yamati. I was sure I couldn't afford him, but I made the appointment anyway.

Joseph recovered that time, but his asthma was not better. One morning before our appointment to see Dr. Yamati it began to rain. I put a sweater on Joseph under his rain slicker. I stuffed a hankie in his pocket and placed a plastic rain hat on his head and an umbrella in his hand. It was not very cold out, and I probably made a mistake by insisting on Joseph's always dressing warmly. This made him sweat and did more harm than good. In any case, Joseph had forgotten his umbrella in school and on his way home he got wet. That evening he had another life-threatening attack.

This time, instead of taking him to the hospital, I called Dr. Yamati. I knew it was probably a waste of time. It was eleven-thirty and I'd yet to meet a doctor who made house calls even at a decent hour. But I called anyway. To my amazement and relief, Dr. Yamati took down directions and said he'd be right over, even though he'd never laid eyes on Joseph or me before.

Dr. Yamati was Oriental. I had never spoken to a Japanese person before and now I was inviting one into my house and hoping he could save my Joseph. He was about the same height as me. He was immaculate and wearing a sport jacket even so late at night. He went into Joseph's room and gave him a couple of shots, then assured us both that Joseph would be just fine now and that he'd feel better in a few minutes. Then he instructed me to give Joseph a hot shower and to get in the shower with him. He showed me how to massage his chest and explained that as Joseph breathed in the steam and I massaged, the mucus would loosen and he'd be able to cough it up. For the first time in years I had the feeling of being taken care of. I thought Dr. Yamati would leave then, but he told me he'd wait in the living room.

After I dried Joseph's hair and tucked him into bed, I made some coffee and Dr. Yamati sat with me in the kitchen. The odd thing was that it didn't feel strange or frightening to have this man sitting there, alone with me. Maybe it was because we were the same size, or maybe it was because he was Japanese and so gentle and unlike the other men I'd known. I wondered if Bill would think it improper for me to be in the house alone with him. Should I have asked my mother to come by? That was ridiculous. It was two in the morning. I wondered if Dr. Yamati was wondering where Joseph's father was. He said, "You have trouble," posed as a statement instead of a question.

I nodded.

"You have fear of your child's illness?"

I nodded again.

"We will make him strong. He'll get better. That I can promise. You're going to have to keep an eye on him. You're going to have to learn to detect an attack before it happens so we can prevent it. But I'll help you with this. Excuse me, but is there no father?"

I shook my head and willed myself not to cry.

"Is this a new development?"

I nodded. "He'll be back in four years."

"So there is an adjustment. In the beginning it's difficult, but you'll adjust. So will Joseph. You'll see. He's a smart boy, I can tell. I don't want you to worry. Your son has an attack, you call me and I'll treat him. Simple. We'll have a treatment routine, and the attacks will be less."

I met his eyes for the first time and he held them, then nodded once, and I knew one thing: Dr. Yamati had been telling me the truth and would always do so. Then and there Dr. Yamati became my hero. I felt I could trust him. It was a lightening of my body, which happened because of the relief of pressure. I would not have to face Joseph's illness alone.

Maybe things were finally looking up. I was sure of it when Gay told me he sold the serial rights for *Honor Thy Father* to *Esquire*. He would be paid forty-five hundred dollars and Bill wanted me to accept the money. I worried that if I accepted it I'd lose my welfare, but was advised by the welfare department that if I spent the money in one month's time I would not lose my monthly allotment. I accepted gratefully. I bought things that might have broken down within the next five years: a refrigerator, a washer and dryer, a stove, and good-quality mattresses. Then I lost my welfare.

So I worked more and summoned every ounce of will and energy stored in my mind and my body to fulfill a promise I'd made long ago: that my children would have a normal life. I was determined they would not be deprived of their childhood because their father was absent. I was singly focused on this task. I drove myself so hard, I hadn't one moment in the day for pleasure. I worked three jobs: full-time at the title-search company, where I'd been promoted to title officer; I gave Rubbermaid demonstrations one or two evenings a week; and I passed out pieces of pies that I'd baked using piña colada or grasshopper mix at supermarkets on Saturdays. To stretch every cent, I didn't just shop at a supermarket, I made extra trips—to the bakery (five loaves of bread for a dollar), the warehouse (discount prices on spaghetti,

canned tomatoes and corn, applesauce, and may-
onnaise), the butcher (top round for fifty-seven
cents a pound, from which I made ground beef; cut
London broil, which I sliced thin for sandwiches;
stew meat; and a roast). The heat was placed at
sixty-two degrees. I figured out every meal to the
morsel and we had no extras. I stayed up every
night until eleven doing the laundry, vacuuming,
sewing Gigi's communion dress. I was determined
that Gigi would have the most beautiful communion dress I could imagine. I created a bodice by
weaving picot ribbon. The sleeves and the skirt
were made of dotted Swiss. I had to keep sending
Gigi out for more ribbon. It ended up costing me
thirty dollars, which was much more than I'd have
paid for a ready-made dress, but this was important.
Plus, I think I wanted to keep myself busy because
I was so anxious I could hardly sleep.

Fear had become a terrible habit.

One day I got up at five-thirty as usual, dressed,
and made my way into the kitchen, quietly so I
wouldn't wake the children. I unloaded the dishwasher, made meat loaf sandwiches (we never had
cold cuts because they were too expensive and not
healthy), then set the table for breakfast, and made
a pot of oatmeal. Next I made little lists for each
of the children: "Joseph: scour the toilet, tub and
sink, put away your laundry" (Thanks to Dr. Yamati, Joseph had started to talk about becoming a
doctor. And indeed he would grow up to become
a pediatrician. I always gave him the disinfecting-
type cleaning jobs because he was the best at it);

"Chuck: mow the lawn and put away your laundry"; "Tore: trim the bushes, empty the dishwasher, sweep the driveway and put away your laundry"; "Gigi: sweep the kitchen floor and put away your laundry." I'd folded their laundry and put it in piles on the washer and dryer the night before. Next, I taped their lists of chores to their plates. There was a time when the first one up would switch around the lists. But I got wise and put their names on them.

Then I woke them up, told them to be good and to study hard in school, not to forget to wash and brush their teeth, and to be kind to each other, then drove off to work. This was the fall of 1972. Chuck was fourteen, Joe eleven, Tore nine, and Gigi eight. I'd been worried about what I'd do with them in the summer. I told my brother and we decided to ask our cousin Nellie's daughter Carla, who was sixteen, to come out for the summer, and my brother bought her ticket. Carla told me that all day every day my kids and half the neighborhood crowded into the garage and played endless games of caroms on a board Nino had found next to a Goodwill bin. Every day after school my mother dropped by on her way home from work at a nursing home just to check on things. Whenever there was an emergency they called Aunt Annie and Uncle Lou, but I still felt guilty. It was difficult for them, I knew. Hard enough to have a father stuck away in jail, maybe harder still to have a mother at work.

I thought of the letter Bill had written me, which

was tucked into my pocketbook beside me on the car seat. He'd been participating in a writing workshop and had sent me a poem he'd written about Gigi:

> I see you in my dreams
> Swimming with calico carps.
> And riding Dalmatian giraffes
> Climbing bougainvillea vines into the
>   skies.
>
> I treasure your happiness
> As you hopscotch in the early rain
> Or tag me with bean bags
> And kiss my bruised neck.

I'd felt emotional when I read it, but this morning it galled me. There he was, off in jail, studying law, writing poetry, contemplating the world, being a regular Renaissance man, while I was out here dealing with the nitty-gritty of the day-to-day. It was almost two years now since he'd left and I still hadn't forgiven him. I felt a wave of exhaustion pass over me. I wished I had time to drop by church and sink into the peace and quiet, but that was impossible. Sundays had had to be enough lately.

Most times I went to mass with one or two of the kids, usually Gigi or Joseph. The other two were too busy playing or puttering around the neighborhood. I'd given up on forcing them. I simply told them I couldn't do it alone, that God was my partner. I explained that on Sundays, I thanked

Him for every blessing: healthy children, our good home, and the good people around us. I asked Him to hold us in the palm of His hand and protect us. I'd say, "Look at it this way. If humans lived on a scale from one to one hundred from animal to divine, I think we should try to live at the seventy-five mark, what do you think?" I doubt they'd ever given me a response. But they were good kids. And they helped me a lot. They became serious about their chores after I'd said, "If people came and saw a messy house, they'd think I was a terrible mother." They had their pride too. I said a prayer for my children as I pulled into the parking lot.

I was worried and morose this morning on my way to work. I forced a smile on my face and kept it there until I parked. Maybe the outward appearance of happiness would lighten me up somehow. No chance. I wasn't at work for two hours before I pushed the wrong button on my computer and started a program that wouldn't abort. We called San Diego. They didn't know how to abort it either. I'd crippled the company. My boss said, "Cheer up. You'll probably get fired but at least you'll go out with distinction. You could write a book: How to sabotage a company in half a second. Don't look so scared. I'm only kidding, only kidding."

Everybody tried to catch up on paperwork until we got our computers back, but it was busy-making work that made us all grouchy. I called home at three-thirty to check up on the kids. Tore answered. "Are you sweeping the driveway?" I said.

"Yes," he said. "I think you should give me money."

I tried to give them an allowance, just a little bit every week, but sometimes something came up, like an extra weekend in a month, and I just didn't have it. Last week had been one of those times. "I thought you did it for love," I said.

"I don't love the driveway, Mom."

"You love me, don't you? And you love God and He wants you to work. What are your brothers and sisters doing?"

"Joseph's at Brett's. Gigi's not here. Chuck's in the garage. Can I go now?"

I called up Annie. Gigi was there playing with her cousin Lia, who was also her best friend. Chuck had taken to buying old lawnmowers, restoring their motors, then fastening them onto planks that he fashioned into go-carts. He had sold two of them already. I knew that Chuck probably wasn't in the garage alone, because he always had an audience. While Tore had been on the phone I heard a chorus of kids in the background. Our house had become the neighborhood hangout and Tore was a ringleader. Our kids were the most popular on the block. I could see they got their winning personalities from their father.

Soon after I'd lost my welfare an Italian documentary maker approached me for an interview for Italian TV. After consulting with Bill I agreed to it, and had been paid one thousand dollars in cash. I used it to buy a secondhand car after looking in the want ads for a month and test-driving a couple of cars a week with Chuck. This was the first big thing I'd ever bought with money I'd earned myself and it was a pretty heady feeling.

The day the film crew parked around our house there'd been a constantly shifting audience of kids and neighbors watching. Naturally, the neighborhood kids thought that anybody who attracted limos and film crews had to be cool, and after that my kids had it made. Then there was the IRS man, poor Mr. Summers, whose job it was to sit in his car all day and keep an eye on our house. The kids threw lemons at him daily. Joseph was studious and quiet by nature and he befriended a boy named Brett who had no brothers or sisters or a father. His mother worked all day and Brett went home to an Italian grandmother after school. She would have a hot meal waiting and Joseph would join his good buddy. I'm sure Joseph's frailty worried the old woman, and little by little she figured out what Joseph's favorite foods were. She bought bags of pistachio nuts and gallons of chocolate chip ice cream to feed him. After spending the afternoon at Brett's, Joseph came home and ate dinner with us at six. Joseph gained thirty pounds in a year, and for the first time in his life he looked healthy.

Sitting in the office praying the computer screen would come back to life, I thought how different my children's lives were from anything I'd ever imagined. Yes, they had clean clothes on their backs and three square meals a day and clean sheets to slip between at bedtime, but they were also forced to be so damned independent. Once they'd broken the picture window playing baseball. They pooled their savings and had it replaced before I came home from work. The only reason I found out about it was because Nino had dropped by while the men were there installing the glass. Bill had also heard of it and was proud of them. The kids wrote Bill every week and Bill wrote back to them, but he was missing their communions and confirmations and graduations from elementary school. I felt sorry for him and sorry for my children. My sister Annie and Louie accompanied me to all ceremonies. They were our guardians. They took us on weekends to their cabin in the mountains and sometimes to picnics in the park. Louie saved me a fortune by cutting my boys' hair. I knew I should consider myself lucky to have such a family, and I did. Louis was Sicilian like us, and he knew Bill before Annie ever met him. He grew up in Brooklyn and was familiar with that *element*, but he'd wanted nothing to do with it. He was a sweet man, and domestic, an excellent cook and father. Bill had often said that he'd married the wrong sister, because Annie was feisty, had a sharp sense of humor, and could argue with Bill anytime, anywhere, for as long as he wanted.

Annie had married a good husband, but I had to admit to myself that as difficult, even horrible, as times could be with my husband around, I ached for him. As it had happened the other times he was gone, the anger faded and I remembered the good times.

At least I didn't have to ache for the computer

anymore because it came back to life at four. I could stop thinking and put some decent work in. Since I felt so guilty for my flap, I stayed until six-thirty and was utterly exhausted by the time I got home and realized I'd forgotten to take the meat out of the freezer that morning. I collapsed into a chair and started bawling. There was nothing else in the house to eat and I was too tired to go to a store to buy something. I'd make some eggs but we needed them for breakfast. There was apple-sauce. Mashed potatoes would take too long. There was pasta of course, but no sauce to put on it. I thought of the other night when I'd awakened and heard someone in the kitchen. I walked in and saw Chuck sneaking a bowl of cereal. I screamed, "Stop eating cereal!" He looked up in shock, dropped his spoon, and we stared at each other, then started laughing.

I wished I could laugh now but it didn't seem funny.

I went to the door and called the kids. They wandered in one by one and no one mentioned dinner. They went straight to the TV.

My body felt like it weighed a ton; I could not lift myself. Maybe I could make myself angry and yelp a karate yell, like I did whenever I had to move something heavy like the refrigerator. Then once I was on my feet I'd figure out what to do next. I heard a knock at the door. It was Brett's grandmother. I opened the door and said, "Come in. Come in." She was holding a big pot filled with spaghetti and meatballs.

"You worked late today," said Mrs. Cusimano. "I saw you drive in. I thought you must be tired. So, I bring you spaghetti. It's not much, but today you have a break from cooking."

That spaghetti, without doubt, was the most delicious meal I've ever eaten. And accepting that generous woman's help marked a turning point in my life.

Things come to you when you most need them. God looks out for you.

Little by little I replaced my defeatist attitude of pessimism with one of optimism. I let people into my house and my heart, people who were different from me and not family. I learned from them, and they gave me a lot to be grateful for. First there had been Christine and Dr. Yamati. Then I was befriended by two divorced women from work. One was remarried and another a single mother, kind of like me. These were people I never would have dreamed of being friends with once upon a time. And there were my neighbors Nancy and Angie.

Angie was a Greek who married an Italian named Ray after her first marriage to a ne'er-do-well failed. Ray and Angie had a marriage I aspired to. They did everything together. They dug holes to plant bushes, using two shovels, standing side by side. They took bike rides together. They knew exactly what they could afford and saved for big expenses such as trips or a car or improvements on the house. She drove the nice car and he drove the clunker. Ray gave her his paycheck and came home to eat every night. Ray was like a brother to me, helping me with this or that plumbing or electric problem. One winter Ray and Angie took us skiing and treated my kids to lessons. They gave me a surprise birthday party in 1973 and always looked out for me and the children. One day, when I was at work, Tore went into a rage at Joseph and chased him into the yard with a baseball bat, and Angie ran over and disarmed him. When she heard more than the usual racket wafting out of my windows she charged right in and acted the sergeant. I could always count on her to give the children a ride home from school when it was raining. We had real "girl" talks. Angie couldn't believe what I didn't know. We giggled and had secrets like in the old days with my sisters and cousins. When she learned I had no idea of the meaning of slang expressions like "horny, "pussy," or "rubbernecking," she was amazed.

Nancy, who lived on the other side, was a college graduate, wore shorts around the house, cooked vegetables from a can, and piled her clean laundry on the couch, where it waited to be folded, sometimes for days.

Nancy couldn't get over my naïveté either. She said, "Rosalie, you're a saint. You're always thinking of your kids' needs before yours, you're always throwing a celebration for a holiday or communion or graduation. Isn't that exhausting and expensive for you? How do you manage all those people in your home?" I would tell her it was very important for me to keep things just as if their dad was here.

Nancy was my biggest fan and I enjoyed her Wasp attitude and she appreciated my old-fashioned ways.

I wondered what Nancy would have thought of the celebrations we used to have when I was a kid, when there would be twenty adults instead of ten and thirty to fifty kids running around, but always quiet and polite in the face of an adult. We knew our place. Our fathers were not the type who would come out and play baseball with us. They were taking care of their own business.

Once when Mr. Bonanno came by, Nancy said, "Rosalie has made some good friends," and he said, "Rosalie has *allowed* you to become her friend." She was mesmerized by his stories from history, tales of his life, and opinions about art. She'd become great pals with Nino, who taught her to drink espresso, and the two of them would sit at her kitchen window for hours talking and keeping an eye on my kids.

I heard from my mother that people said I was getting too friendly with the neighbors. I wondered who had filed that report, which made me think that as hard as I might try, there was no way I'd ever really be a regular American. People were noticing the change in me. I wouldn't let that stop me. I read some self-help books and magazine articles that encouraged me to think positively and to act as if I had everything the way I wanted. I'd done much thinking about Bill and me. We were very different. Our big mistake was our wanting the other person to be like ourselves. I would stop that.

I'd give Bill more freedom. He was a gregarious and popular person, while I had wanted him to be more reclusive and exclusive, like me. I decided that when he came home I would think of him more as a public person, an actor or a congressman whom I'd have to share with other people. I would continue to build and improve my life so I wouldn't be dependent solely on Bill for my self-satisfaction. I wouldn't expect too much so I wouldn't get hurt.

I thought of myself as a modern woman and possessed a new self-confidence. I'd been promoted to title officer at my company and actually had people working under me. I made enough money with my three jobs to hire a Mexican gardener to plant a lawn and make a path of rocks in the backyard. I now wore jeans and shorts with sneakers. I was thin and attractive and tanned. Bill told me I looked pretty during one of our visits.

The children and I averaged a visit a month with Bill. We ate breakfast at five, then packed a lunch and piled into the car. We started our journey by saying, "Dear God, our lives are in your hands, amen." I sat with Chuck in the front seat and tried to keep peace by doling out M&M's at a rate of one every twenty miles while Chuck drove. When we began this routine Chuck was only fifteen and had a driver's permit.

The sadness never diminished no matter how many times I saw Bill approach us in his khaki trousers with the drawstring waist and those heavy army-type shoes. Bill was a sharp and fussy dresser. He wore tailored slacks, shirts of natural fibers, expensive Italian shoes. I wondered if it hurt Bill to have us see him that way.

I know it hurt him to see the children growing taller and smarter with each visit. He was missing so much. Sometimes he confided his sadness to me in letters. Sometimes he sent me his poems, which spoke often of love.

Bill had done well in prison. He'd even published an article about playing tennis in *Tennis Magazine* for which he was paid one hundred dollars. When he sent me that check and I realized it was the first check I'd seen with his name written on it, it brought tears to my eyes. I bought a little telephone table with the money, so that whenever I looked at it I'd be reminded that my husband had earned it despite being locked in prison.

On what would turn out to be our last visit, I dressed extra casually to give him an idea of how much I'd changed. I wore sandals with small heels, dangling earrings, a big bauble of a ring on my finger that Chuck had made in jewelry class, tight jeans, and a scoop-necked pink jersey. As usual, when I saw him approaching I didn't know where to look. It was always embarrassing to meet his eyes. I knew that once we sat down to talk we wouldn't kiss or hold hands or even let our knees touch. Since sex was not allowed us, it was less painful to act as though it did not exist.

The boys shook Bill's hand. Gigi kissed him. "So when are you kids going to stop growing? You give me a shock every time I lay eyes on you."

"We made it in six and a half hours," Chuck said.

"You weren't speeding, were you?"

"No. Ask Ma."

"She was looking out the window. How would she know?" Bill teased.

"I was not," I said.

"Dad! I didn't speed," Chuck said. He only half knew his father was teasing.

"All right, all right, son. Just keep your eyes on the road."

"I slept at Lia's house last night, then had to get up at *five* to come home this morning," said Gigi.

"You sleep at her house every night, don't you?" Bill asked.

"No. She sleeps at mine too."

"I can't separate those girls," I said.

Bill shrugged. "Don't you remember you and your cousins?"

My girl cousins hadn't spoken to me since *Honor Thy Father* came out. They'd married into the same world, and they and their families didn't like Bill's exposing the way we lived to the public.

"I'm going to try out for baseball," Tore said. "I'll be the best on the team."

"Just try your hardest. And remember you're a Bonanno," Bill said. "You can do anything you put your mind to."

"Grandpa came to visit last week," Joe said.

"I know. How's he looking?"

"Good," Joe said. "He gave us each ten dollars."

"Don't spend it all in one place."

"I think we're starving," said Gigi.

"Ro, did you bring some change?"

I handed Bill a fistful. "I just happen to have a few quarters," he said, passing them out.

After our children took off across the room toward the vending machines, Bill and I sat down. "You know why they really want those quarters, don't you?"

"Yes," I said. There were couples all over each other, practically having sex in plain view, and the kids liked nothing better than to watch them.

"Don't worry, Rosalie. Just think of it as Sex Education one-oh-one."

"But Gigi. It bothers me."

"What do you want to do? Make her sit still for four hours?"

"No."

"Relax. Just let go. You can't control everything in life. You got to roll with the punches. So do they. Sometimes I think you refuse to see what's in front of your face. You don't accept the reality. Do you mean to tell me you never noticed what's going on around here? Look. Look at that couple."

The woman had a long skirt on and was sitting in her husband's lap. He had his face buried in her chest and they were obviously in the middle of making love.

"It won't be long now, will it?" I said.

"No," he said thoughtfully and not smiling. "It won't."

"I've changed, you know."

"You say that. I know you think that. But tell me how."

"I don't know. I've been alone for three and a half years. I've fended for myself and the kids. I like my job. I have new friends. Will it change when you get out?"

"What do you think? Of course it will."

"Are you worried?" I asked him.

"About what?"

"That it won't work."

"That's something we decide, isn't it? It's up to us. If we want it to work it works."

"Sometimes I worry."

"You like to worry."

I considered this and it was true. "I want it to be good this time."

"I do too," he said. "We'll start over. It is possible, you know. I wrote a new poem. Want to hear?"

I nodded. I loved Bill's poems.

"It's called 'With You,' " he said, then read:

> The road had been rocky,
> with stumbling stones . . .
> competition,
> frustration,
> failure.
>
> I traveled alone most of the time.
> I enjoyed and thrived on this,
> but there were times
> when I became lonely.

I finally realized that companionship
and love could enrich my life,
help me be more complete.

A sunset, a candlelit room, soft music
are so much more now,
with you.

On the ride home I was ambivalent and didn't
know why. I put my finger on the feeling. It was
fear. If Bill didn't make me happy, would I do
something about it?

He would change my life, I had no doubt, but
how?

CHAPTER 13

I dressed in a yellow halter dress and cascaded yards and yards of yellow ribbon from the beams of the living-room ceiling and made yellow bows that we stuck on the windows, the furniture, on bushes. I stretched a ribbon across the driveway, tying one end to a telephone pole and the other to a tree that wasn't old or an oak but would have to do. The kids were lookouts, and when they saw Bill drive up they signaled to me and I blared the "Tie a Yellow Ribbon Round the Ole Oak Tree" song out the window, then ran onto the lawn to watch Bill's face as he drove into the driveway. He was laughing. Gigi and Lia jumped up and down and screamed. The boys ran behind the car and thumped their fists on the back fender.

I watched Bill as he got out of the car and everyone made room for his father to greet him. His father hugged him, then kissed him on both cheeks and turned to the crowd. "I welcome my son," he said, and everyone applauded. Then Bill was mobbed by other relatives and friends. Annie came up beside me and put her arm around my shoulder and squeezed. "It'll be fine, old girl," she said. "You look beautiful." I wrapped my arm around her and squeezed her back. I waited for Bill to find me.

I observed him as he moved from one person to the next, holding their hands, kissing the women on the cheek, smiling and talking. I marveled how Bill could always find something to talk about. Gigi stuck close by, hugging Bill's waist as he rested his hand on her neck. Tore walked backward in front of him through the crowd. Chuck walked along next to Gigi. "Where's Joseph?" Bill asked.

He was off reattaching a bow that had fallen from a bush.

"Get over here, Joe," he yelled. Joseph ran over and stood next to Chuck, fussing with the bow. He was fourteen and up to his father's shoulder already. Chuck was sixteen and almost as tall as Bill.

It was wonderful to make a celebration of Bill's returning, but part of me wanted him to myself. Just Bill and me and our kids getting reacquainted. Then I reminded myself of the reason I had made the celebration. Bill was the type of person who needed people around him, and this was his day, after all. I'd asked the more than twenty people I'd invited to chip in for food, but word got back to my father-in-law, who was annoyed and embarrassed that I'd done such a thing. The morning of the party a crate of lobsters and a bag of shrimp arrived, along with bottles of every type of liquor. There would be chicken and pasta too. I couldn't wait until Bill saw all the seafood, his favorite. He was talking to his cousin Nino now. I must be patient. This was what it was like in my husband's world. He was like a diplomat. I mustn't resent sharing him.

It was also Gigi's birthday, and later there'd be a cake. Bill was released a year early with five years' probation. That this was Gigi's birthday I took as a good omen. I snapped myself out of my reverie and stopped mooning after my husband's attention. I walked out back to start the fire. I poured some charcoal into the barbecue I'd bought Bill as a homecoming present. I had big plans for that barbecue. Bill was going to become a regular chef. He'd grill chickens and steaks and hot dogs and hamburgers while I made a salad and boiled corn on the cob in the kitchen. I had so many domestic pictures stored in my mind, they could last a lifetime.

My mother spied me squirting lighter fluid on the coals and came running out. "It's too much. Where's Louie? He knows how. You don't want to be cooking on this thing. You'll spoil your pretty dress." My mother already had an apron on. She'd brought over the makings for a salad and a couple of grocery bags of soda for the kids. When I saw her carrying them from her car, I'd yelled at her, "Ma, let the boys help." She was fifty-eight and as strong and independent as always. Now that she lived in California she learned to drive and she went to work. She loved her job as activities director at the nursing home. I kissed her on the cheek, and she said, "What?"

My mother-in-law came out wiping her hands on her apron. "*La salsa è fatta,*" she said. "The chickens. They're cut in half. You want me to cut smaller pieces?"

"Yeah, it's better, don't you think?" my mother answered before I had a chance.

Obviously I wasn't needed in the food department.

I went off to look for my brother-in-law and realized I was trembling. I was acting like little Rosalie Profaci at a picnic at Uncle Joe's farm, wishing Bill would notice me, while I thought I'd grown into a confident adult and modern woman. I walked back through the house and out the front door. I took one of Gigi's hands off her father's waist and held it. Finally, our eyes met. "So, what do you think of our birthday girl?" I asked Bill, looking him straight in the face.

"She's a beauty," he said, smiling and looking at her.

"Just like her mother," Don, a neighbor Bill and I had been friendly with before Bill went away, said.

"Yes," Bill said, "Gigi looks like the Labruzzo side of my family. I think she must've grown two feet in three years. What've you been feeding these kids, Ro?"

"Meat loaf!" Gigi and Joe both moaned.

"What?" Bill said, "You want steak?"

"Yeah," they all yelled.

"Nino," Bill called to his cousin, "go get steaks. Steaks for everybody."

There must have been nearly thirty people, family and neighbors. I almost said, "Bill, we've got lobsters, chicken, shrimp, too much," but stopped myself.

I had no idea where he'd gotten the two one-hundred-dollar bills he took from his pocket. By now I knew I hadn't a prayer of figuring out where he got the money, and the truth was, I didn't want to know. I didn't want it to be this way again, Bill impressing everyone with his genosity while I scrimped and saved and worried in the background. Peeling hundred-dollar bills out of your pocket was typical for Bill, but not typical in the world I fancied I now lived in. I stopped myself. I remembered all the lessons I'd learned from my reading about successful relationships. Bill was different from me. If I was going to be happy with him, I'd have to accept him the way he was. Bill needed people around him who would be unconditionally committed to him, who were even prepared to die for him. In his absence I'd just forgotten what he was like. I'd adjust. I'd appreciate him without judging. Bill was a generous man. He liked to treat people and to have a good time. His motto was spend now, worry later. Was that so bad? To some it was good.

"You look younger now than when he left," Don said as we both stood a little distance away and watched Bill hug his aunt.

"What a nice thing to say," I said, smiling at Don, then thinking how wonderful Bill looked. He must have lost thirty pounds in prison and was in terrific shape from playing tennis. I wanted to tell Bill how beautiful he was, but that would come later.

People didn't leave until late in the evening, and when Bill and I finally went to bed it was without ceremony. We simply turned off the lights and lay next to each other. Bill said, "What a day," and soon I heard his breathing turn rhythmic and knew he was sleeping. The sound of his breathing kept me awake. I was not used to it. I remembered his telling me that when a man hasn't had it for a long time, he can't do it. In a way I was relieved. It had been so long since we'd made love, I was sure I'd lost the knack. I couldn't recall what the feelings were like. Eventually I fell asleep, until Bill reached over in the middle of the night and I woke up.

I was hooked all over again.

And so began some of the happiest days of my marriage.

Near the end of his prison stay Bill had published an editorial in *The New York Times* about the failure of the prison system to reform people and about his own plans to walk the straight and narrow. I read it over and over during those early days. It filled me with optimism. Here's part of it:

> . . . My perception of our correctional system prior to my incarceration was one of punishment and corruptness, with public pronouncements of rehabilitation bogus. Now, after being in the belly of the monster, I do not alter my concept one iota. The system's interplay at every level—from the lofty judiciary to the correctional officer walking the tiers

and making bed checks—is one of moral bankruptcy.

I have not seen any change in the system while I have been in prison, a term that started before Attica. I cite that as a benchmark, for never before has the public been exposed to as much stark truth about the inadequacies of the system, and never before has there been such a clamor for reform. But things are now back to normal, and the correctional system that corrects no one of nothing goes on as always: deceit, disparity in sentences, bureaucratic inertia, administrative apathy, ostrich policies, false perspectives being but a few of the combustible elements which will kindle the flame of more Atticas. And little will be done to change it. . . .

I am reasonably intelligent and educated enough to realize what I must do. Since rehabilitation is an admitted failure and a fraud insofar as the correctional system is concerned, for each individual straddled by the system rehabilitation must be self-motivated, desired. For most, perhaps, the motivation and desire is lacking. Not so in my particular case. Too many years have I been plagued with harassment by the law, legitimate or otherwise, by a sense of fidelity to an ancient mystique and heritage, by a desire to fulfill, if not predestined, at least a prescribed philosophy of life.

Melodramatic as I may sound, there is an

almost desperate need for me to veer drastically from old paths to new horizons which are best for me and my family to enjoy in relative peace and comfort, comfort of self and peace of mind.

Evolution and changes in the socio-economic life style of my ethnic heritage very clearly show that if I am to survive, I must become part of that evolution. I recognize that now is the time I must decide, in spite of the experience of having lived through almost three years of a void, spiritually, morally and physically, what happens to my wife, what happens to my children and, perhaps less importantly, what happens to myself. The chance to resume a normal relationship—as soon as possible—and to be integrated into society, is the key to rehabilitation and the answer to the recidivism problem, not only for me but for all men and women living in these concrete monuments to society's indifference and the system's failure.

I latched on to the statement "the chance to resume a normal relationship." At last Bill wanted what I wanted. He had met Angie and Ray, and liked them. We spent some Sundays sitting by their pool in their backyard sipping lemonade and just relaxing. The four of us, joking and talking, while our kids jumped in and out of the pool. Nancy had invited Bill and me to dinner, and I'd invited her and her husband too. Bill had been charming and interesting, a husband to be proud of. He could have a conversation with anybody about anything. In a way I was showing him off.

This was all new to me. Never before had Bill met my friends. Never before did I have friends. And now Bill had a job that paid him every week. It was as an advertising public relations director for a construction company, for which he brought home $350 in an honest-to-God paycheck every week. This totaled $1,400 a month!

I had not broached the subject of my job with Bill, and when the first workday morning rolled around, I awoke nervous as a cat. I've never needed an alarm clock, and when I could sense it was five-thirty, I sat up in bed slowly and quietly. I jumped when I felt Bill's hand holding me in bed by the shoulder.

"Where do you think you're going?" he said.

"To work," I said.

"Oh, yeah? And who told you you could go to work?"

"Nobody."

He pulled me back into the bed and kissed me. "I think you're going to have to pay for that privilege."

"Bill, I'll be late," I said, squirming away from underneath him.

He pinned my arms and my legs and said, "Stay."

I stopped moving. I said, "Bill?"

He let me go and slapped me on the behind as

I got out of bed. "Go on," he laughed. "Better not be late or you'll get fired."

I prepared breakfast and lunch for the kids as usual, except for extra bacon and two more eggs for Bill, which I left warming in the oven. I did not tape chores to the kids' plates. I was afraid Bill would use their having to do too much work as a reason to make me quit my job.

I was surprised when I returned home to find the tabled cleared and the dishes in the washer.

"Who did this?" I asked Joseph.

"All of us. Dad made us."

My new husband was full of surprises, and I loved him.

There were nights when Bill brought home a mountain of tacos from Taco Bell and dumped them in the middle of the table, then said, "Dig in." The kids' faces looked as though it were Christmas. The only time we ate out while Bill was away was when we went to a stand that served five hamburgers for a dollar. We each got one. Now Bill not only brought home two dozen tacos, he brought French fries and every type and flavor of soft drink on the menu. "Where're your cousins?" he said, meaning Annie's kids. "Call them up. We got tacos coming out of our ears here." Tore and Joe raced to the phone. Tore won and called his cousins.

To me, Bill was simply great. He organized a fundraiser for Tore's Yellow Jackets football team, which made the evening news. He interceded with Chuck's English teacher to hammer out a schedule that would allow Chuck to make up work he'd done poorly on, and so not be held back. He went to Joe's Little League games and Tore's Yellow Jackets games. He went to parent-teacher conferences when I couldn't. The kids were proud of their father. In fact, Bill was now something of a local celebrity: *Honor Thy Father* had sold millions, and the media, like me, were interested in how Bill was planning to lead his life now that prison and the "Banana Wars" were behind him. They featured him in the local papers and on TV. He told them he was looking for a publisher for the poetry he'd written in prison and that he was considering writing a sequel to *Honor Thy Father*.

Soon Bill was on the lecture circuit, where he traveled to college campuses, talked about his life, and was paid for each lecture, which the Internal Revenue Service seized. Then the IRS approached his regular employer, and Bill decided to quit rather than have them harassed. My fantasy world began to crumble. Once more, no regular job.

Now that he had so much free time, he decided we should take a trip as a family. The last time we'd done anything like that was when we'd sailed the channels of the Sacramento before Bill went to prison. It had been fun, if scary, and had brought us closer together, but I couldn't just up and take off from my job. Bill suggested we take a trip to revisit the places we used to drive to when we lived in Flagstaff, then go spend time with his mother and father in Tucson. He insisted, "Life is too short. Get your priorities straight. Your boss doesn't want you to go? Quit the goddamned job."

My boss was a patient and understanding man. I had two weeks' vacation coming and he gave me two more without pay. I tried my best to warn him, though, that I couldn't promise I'd be back when expected.

Driving in a camper with our four kids for a month on the road was one thing, but bringing Tinker, our unpredictable and neurotic little dog, was another. This dog was a classic. It attacked postmen, kids, other dogs, and anything that moved. I didn't want him walking from one room to another with me, so I certainly didn't want him taking a trip with us. But the kids whined and Bill declared the monster one of us. I was beginning to remember the way nothing stays calm when Bill is around.

So what happened the first time we made a pit stop? Tinker chased another camper in the opposite direction and we had to wait ten minutes while Bill chased him down the road. As far as Bill and my kids were concerned, that dog was family and family meant for life. No matter how much trouble that dog got into or hurt it caused, they would never consider giving it up. That sense of loyalty is one of the best qualities Bill has instilled in our children, which I'm grateful for, but personally, I drew the line with dogs.

While we were on our trip, Bill decided it was time to face the IRS and try to free us from this albatross. They said we owed $165,471 in unpaid taxes for 1965–1967. With penalties and interest our debt now totaled $344,540.

In an attempt to free us from that debt in the event that we might one day make some real legitimate money, Bill went to bankruptcy court to prove that our assets were nothing but my job. And so I was thrown right back into court, where I had to testify about my job and how much money I made. This was my third appearance. Early in our marriage I'd had to take the stand and talk about having no money, and another time I'd had to testify in front of a grand jury, asserting that I knew basically nothing about my husband's life, which had been at its best embarrassing and at its worst demeaning.

I hid in my usual oblivion. Except for the days I actually physically had to be in court, I ignored the whole thing.

Now Bill was home most of the time. He concentrated on this or that promise of a Hollywood career, the possibility of a sequel to Gay's book, and the opening of a book-publishing company, which would publish books written by other people. He was collaborating with a talented writer he'd met in prison and they were planning literary projects.

Bill had become fairly downcast. He was annoyed at my being occupied with other things. Nothing was happening the way he'd hoped. My optimism began to look more and more like a bubble that was about to burst. I said, "Bill, you're reaching too high. Your problem is your reputation precedes you. Why can't you just live a simple life?" He ignored me.

He was jealous of my being occupied with other things. He began to put me down. When he watched me get ready for work in the morning, he said, "Oh, Christ, not the electric curlers. If you didn't spend so much time in the mirror you might look a little natural. You wear too much goddamned makeup." Then he started a new game. Every time we went somewhere in the car he'd test me. He'd turn on a classical station and say, "So, Ro, what's the name of this aria?"

"I don't know."

"What do you mean, you don't know? You must've heard it a hundred times. Listen to it. All right, all right. Where is it from? Just guess."

"I don't know."

"It's 'La donna è mobile' from *Rigoletto* by Giuseppe Verdi. All right. So you've forgotten your opera this morning. How about something popular." Then he switched the station. "Well, what's the name of this one?"

"I don't know, Bill."

" 'Days of Wine and Roses.' How could you not know that? Jesus, how did you get so stupid? I don't know how the hell you graduated high school."

Now when I went to work, I had to have every dish and piece of laundry done before I walked out the door or he wouldn't let me leave. He'd say, "For you, working's a privilege. You want to do it, you'll have to work twice as hard for the opportunity."

One time he called me at work and told me to come home immediately. I had visions of hurt children, a fire in the kitchen. What I found at home were some out-of-town people who'd dropped by. My priorities should be cooking for Bill and guests. Bill couldn't stand the idea of his wife's not being there to serve. What would it look like? Bill's attitude was beginning to frighten me. I did not want him to force me to drop what I'd worked so hard for. To be able to take care of myself and my kids was the main source of my new self-esteem.

Finally the court ruled on the bankruptcy. I was discharged from all previous debt, but Bill was still responsible. To Bill this was a legal victory because we'd set a precedent. His attitude changed overnight. Suddenly it was fine with him that I worked. He even asked me how my days went. He was more cheerful. We opened a store that sold polyester tops and pants. I had good enough credit to borrow the money. I hoped one day I could quit my job and we'd work together. But the store went broke.

In spite of everything, Bill was a good parent. The kids' schoolwork had improved since he came home. Bill made a point of asking them about it, which encouraged them to have more pride and interest. Chuck was already a junior in high school and had invented a uniski by putting two footholds on one narrow ski. But at the slopes they thought it too dangerous, and once he skied at a place, he was usually forbidden to return, so he worked as a mechanic to finance his trips to a different slope every weekend. Joseph went to Bellarmine High School, which was Jesuit and very rigorous academically. (We paid his tuition with an educational trust fund Gay Talese and Bill had set up out of the profits of some of the subsidiary rights to *Honor Thy Father*.) Tore was twelve now and had broken his heel for the third time playing football, although it didn't quell his rambunctiousness any. He was actually turning out to be a kind, considerate, strong-minded boy. Gigi was eleven and had an outgoing personality. She had a job caring for three small children in the neighborhood, and word of her abilities had spread so that she had more baby-sitting jobs than she could handle.

I worried so much about them, perhaps I was overly strict about curfews. If they had any tendencies like their father's, which was to go with the flow and seize chances as soon as they came up and not worry about the consequences, I wanted to nip them in the bud.

Sometimes I wondered who I was. I loved being a career person but I also got actual pleasure from ironing a shirt and seeing Bill wear it. And I could understand his wanting me home to serve his friends. Sitting around a meal and digesting food to good conversation was one of life's pleasures, and I liked contributing to that pleasure. I used to resent entertaining because I felt like a slave, but now it seemed like a wonderfully social thing to do, a way to share. To break bread with friends. To make memories. Was I the docile woman who lived with Bill and did as he wished, or the organized and efficient woman who did a good job at her work and even told other people what to do sometimes?

I wondered where Bill and I were going. We both wanted the same thing, but he wanted it his way and I wanted it mine. I felt we were building a wall between us, not a bridge. On this one point I was sure: I did not want to live as the ignored and used wife of Bill Bonanno. I would be his wife if he would be my husband. I wanted him to love me, truly, or let me go.

Soon after Bill came home from prison we began going out to dinner with our friends April and Don—Don was recuperating from surgery. Lately he had been dropping by when I came home from work. We sat out back, drank coffee, and talked. I liked Don. He was a gentleman to his wife, and he seemed sensitive and particularly interested in what I had to say. He always rinsed out his cup before he left and sometimes he brought over flowers he'd picked or some lemons from his tree. He was a Catholic who went to church almost as often as I did. We went to the Lenten Mission at our church. On Saturday mornings too, sometimes, Don stopped over and again we talked: about our childhoods, how I fell in love with Bill, how he fell in love with April, his wife.

I knew Bill would not approve of my friendship with Don, but looking back on it, I think I was trying to force my hand. To bring something to a head.

One night Bill was out of town and Don's wife

wasn't due home with his kids until nine, so Don stayed for dinner with me and the kids. My children went out afterward and Don helped me clean up the kitchen. As I was wiping down the table, he took hold of my wrist.

Surprised, I looked up at him.

He pulled me to him and our lips almost touched.

"You have such beautiful eyes. From the first time I saw them I've been bewitched by you."

It felt dangerous, forbidden. Wonderful. I had never kissed anyone but Bill in my life. Don was much smaller. His beard was rough. I was excited. He tried to kiss me and I felt him press against me. I came to my senses and pulled away.

"What?" he said.

"It's wrong."

"No, it's not."

"I'm married. You're married. It's a sin."

"You are a beautiful woman. You know how to make a man feel important."

I was losing control. I was afraid of what I felt. Guilt stopped me short.

Just then Bill's cousin Nino walked in. What he saw could have just been Don and me standing in my kitchen talking. But something about the way we looked, or just the fact that we were alone together, made him suspicious.

I was relieved when Bill confronted me. This was it. Either he'd let me go or he'd work harder to keep me.

"What's this I hear about you and Don?" Bill said.

"He's a friend. He pays attention to me. He likes me."

"How many times did you let this *credino* in my house?"

"I don't know. We're just friends. Bill, he's company. He listens. He doesn't think I'm stupid."

"You are so goddamned naïve. You think any man's going to come over here just to listen to you?"

"I suppose."

"You suppose," he mimicked me. "He never tried anything?"

I looked at my lap and shook my head.

"You let that wimp over here? Around my kids? Since when is it all right to invite men in my house?"

"I don't know," I said. I felt guilty. Bill was my husband. I was in love with Bill. I wanted him to love me back. I suppose that was what Don and I had been all about. I wanted Bill to know that I was lovable, that another man was attracted to me.

I told Bill I didn't love Don, only him. I confessed about the attempted kiss.

That was a mistake. He wanted to run down the road and kill him.

I realized what a powder keg I'd played with.

I begged him to have sense. What about our kids? Don's wife? Don's kids? Somehow I calmed him.

Bill never did confront Don because I think he

was afraid that if he laid eyes on him he'd kill him.
But somehow it was conveyed to Don that he was
never to set foot in our house again.

My plan either to be set free or to make Bill
realize how much he loved me backfired. Instead,
Bill got back at me but good.

When the clothing business failed he started a
construction firm. He needed a secretary, so I rec-
ommended a young girl who'd just been let go
from the title company. Her name was Donna. She
became his private secretary. She was nineteen.

I knew what was happening when Bill began to
come home later and later and sometimes not at
all. He was out of town "on business." When I
heard from Donna's friend who worked with me at
the title company that Donna had moved out of her
parents' house and into an apartment of her own, I
accused Bill of having an affair with his secretary.
He went into a rage and denied it. I didn't persist
because I was too afraid of the accusations he
would fling back at me. He referred to me and Don
as "that thing." I was getting tired of going to bed
alone.

There were some weekends when I didn't see
Bill at all. When I'd ask where he'd been, he'd say,
"Out of town," or he wouldn't answer. All the other
nights he came home to sleep for a few hours, as
though he were making certain that at least I
couldn't accuse him of not coming home to sleep.
Maybe he did it for the children. This was an improvement over Erica times, but not much of one.

It was as though my indiscretion had let out the

rage he'd kept under control since we lived at my uncle Magliocco's. I was constantly on guard. There was no telling what would set off a tantrum. He broke a wrought-iron ironing board in half during one of them.

I had a couple of places where I went to pray. One was a prayer room at the Bethel Church. It wasn't Catholic, but it was brand new and near my mother's house. At their opening they'd passed out keys to a tiny room that contained only two benches and a cross. It was quiet and dimly lit, peaceful and calming in its austerity. Other times I drove to the top of Mount Montalvo, where the city had turned an old estate into a park. I walked through the paths there and asked God to reveal his will to me.

There was a point on the mountain where you could see from Gilroy to San Francisco. I often sat there. Once I closed my eyes and remembered a scene from when my father was alive. I must have been thirteen or fourteen when I decided I was going to pull out a bunch of rocks where our property met the road up in Cornwall. Nature was too disorganized for me. I wanted to make it symmetrical. I planned to lay a stone path to our porch and to border it with flowers. I dug all day from morning to night and was stricken with the worst poison ivy imaginable. I had it on every inch of my body. It was in my nose, my eyes, between my toes. My mother painted me with calamine lotion and I lay puffed up, itchy, and stiff in bed when my father came home from work. He quietly took one step into my room, looked at me on the bed, and started to cry. That was the only time I ever saw him shed a tear. To me, sitting on that mountain, it meant that he'd loved me. I wished he were still with me. I wondered if things would be different if he were still alive.

I never confided these problems to my mother or my brother. I didn't want my mother to hate Bill, nor did I want her to worry. If I told my brother how things were deteriorating, I was afraid he'd feel he had to do something. Then there'd be a fight. I did not want to put him in that position again.

Things had become worse.

My friends at work and my relatives saw Bill and his girlfriend all over town, at lunches, at dinners, shopping in stores, driving in Bill's car. I felt that he was punishing me for my indiscretion by flaunting his. At first people mentioned this casually. Then not at all. They were too embarrassed. I confronted Bill, and this turned him into a madman.

Bill adhered to the philosophy that the best defense is a good offense. He locked me in our bedroom. "Why you think I'm having an affair? Who told you? People at work? Maybe you'd better quit that goddamned job. Remember, Rosalie, whenever you point a finger at me you have three fingers pointing back at yourself. Maybe you're so suspicious because I should be suspicious of you."

I didn't know how to react. If I became angry he became angrier. If I remained silent he called me a martyr. He went on and on until he broke me. Until I was so drained I'd say anything, agree to anything, to shut him up. "I was wrong," I said. "You're not having an affair with Donna. She's your secretary. You *have* to spend a lot of time together."

Once he believed he had control of me, as soon as he saw me limp and spiritless, we made love. He won me back body and soul. Or so he thought.

After one of these fights, I controlled my accusations for a month, maybe two, until I could repress neither my pain, my frustration, nor my tongue another second. Our last fight was the worst. I screamed. I begged. "Please just let me go. You can have her. You found yourself a nice young girl. An Italian. You'll be happier. I've never been good for you. I don't understand you. Donna does. She admires you. The way you are. Whatever you do out there, she understands and applauds it. The kids are practically grown. They can handle it. I'm still at an age when I can start a new life. Let me go!"

"What does that mean, new life?" he asked.

"I don't know. Over again."

"I don't understand. 'Over again'? What do you mean? That's what I hate about you. Can't you just explain yourself? Look, you're clamming up. Just tell me what's on your mind."

"I don't know," I repeated. I knew Bill too well to fall into this trap. If I'd said "Find a new husband," he would have gone berserk.

"Over again, doing what?" he insisted.

"I don't know," I insisted.

"What do you mean, you don't know? You said it. You must've meant something."

My husband was brought up by his father to be a warrior. He views the world in terms of offense and defense. His maneuvers are usually meant to keep people off balance to gain advantage for himself. Mostly through fear. Lies and deception are simply part of his repertoire, a means to an end. So is switching from rage to charm. His philosophy is the end justifies the means. I, on the other hand, had been taught to be lovable, self-denying, and submissive. In other words, a martyr. Without knowing it I was the perfect victim.

This last battle ended with Bill's locking me in the bedroom for three days. He believed that when there was a major problem you just stopped life and took care of it. I couldn't go to work or even shopping for food. Once when I tried to sneak out, he cut up my favorite dress with scissors in front of my face and said, "You're not going anywhere." He took care of the kids and didn't leave the house. He made me call in sick. By the end of this ordeal, my head was bowed, my shoulders sagged, and my voice was no louder than a whisper.

"The truth is, Rosalie," he said when he brought back my clothes. "I don't think I love you enough to let you go." Then he told me he'd made reservations for me to go stay with his aunt in Florida. "You need a vacation. Go straighten out your head."

And that's what I did.

I saw it all, clear as a picture. Bill didn't love

me and he never had. Back at Uncle Magliocco's, when he'd seduced me again with all the attention and the gifts, it had been for the sake of appearances, for form. That's probably why he liked to see me pregnant too. It looked good. It gave the impression of a happy marriage to the world. Something turned off in my heart.

I prayed to God to help me forgive Bill. I talked to the kids on the phone every day. I called my mother to assure her that I was just getting a breather and some sun. When my brother Sal called, I assured him of the same thing. We talked only for a short time and said nothing significant. I would regret this two days later when my mother called to tell me he was dead. He'd died of a heart attack in his home.

I wept on the plane to New Jersey and stared in a stupor at the moon, white on the water, which had a border of twinkling lights all the way up the coast.

I pictured Sal shaking hands with Bill outside Uncle Joe Magliocco's office after Bill had threatened my brother with a gun in our mother's house. Sal had looked worried that day shaking hands. There was a smile on his face but it had been insincere. After that his smile had always been forced in Bill's presence. The two men avoided each other whenever possible. My husband included my brother in his scorn for the Profaci cousins who hadn't come to Uncle Magliocco's aid. Bill, I knew, thought they were too busy protecting their assets. My brother, he said, wanted to play it safe.

I think my brother, like me, may have wanted out of that world we'd been born into, but being a boy it had been harder. I remembered how I'd resented Sal's male privileges, the way he had respect because of his sex, while I'd had none. Maybe I'd been the luckier one.

Back when we were children, my brother and Bill had been friends. Because first-born boys of Sicilian families are named after their grandfather, whenever a group of cousins got together there'd be a whole passel of kids with the same name. My husband used to tell the story of the night he went riding around Brooklyn with a group of my cousins. Whoever was driving ran a red light and a cop pulled them over. He shone a flashlight at their faces and said to the five of them, "What're your names?" They said, afraid the cop might get steamed and think them wise guys but telling the truth anyway, "Salvatore Profaci, Salvatore Profaci, Salvatore Profaci, Salvatore Profaci, Salvatore Bonanno."

"Go ahead," the cop waved them on. "My name's Salvatore too."

I wished things had stayed the same. That we'd all stayed close, my brother and the rest of us. But things had fallen apart.

My brother had helped me through the years. There had been a surprise check in the mail once in a while, always when I needed it most, to buy shoes for the kids or winter jackets. He'd sent our sixteen-year-old cousin, who became my savior that first summer Bill was in jail. And there were the phone calls, sometimes once a week. Just checking. Now there would be no more phone calls. No more head of my family. I felt bad for my mother. Her husband had been only forty-nine when he died, and her son forty-two. She'd lost her protectors. I wished I could call Bill and have him console me. I saw how in a healthy marriage my brother's death would have made us feel closer. But that was out of the question. There were old animosities. Deep wounds.

Bill took Joseph out of school in San Jose to escort me to the funeral in New Jersey.

When I arrived home, Bill told me he was facing probation-violation charges. I was commanded to appear in court again. Nothing unusual. Same testimony. How much money I made on my job. No, I had never seen a check from any of my husband's businesses. Yes, as far as I knew there had been no profit. There would be endless hours of listening to lawyers argue over two words for two days. But this time it was no bankruptcy court. This was a criminal trial. Bill had left blank the space on a form where he was asked by the parole board to fill in his income. If the court ruled that this was a form of lying about his income, Bill would go back to jail for probation violation.

I didn't understand him. Was he looking for trouble?

I couldn't ask him this if I wanted to. We were barely speaking. I had to miss work to sit in court and appear to the world like a supportive, concerned wife, while I watched Donna fill his glass with water and peel off Life Savers from a roll in her purse and lay them in the palm of his hand. She carried his papers in every morning, and would leave during the proceedings to make phone calls and then return, whispering whatever information she'd garnered into Bill's ear.

I was so mad, I couldn't eat. Especially when I was required to accompany Bill and Donna and the lawyers and whoever had testified on Bill's behalf to daily lunches and dinners. Bill's treat, of course.

In August 1978 Bill was interned at the federal penitentiary at McNeil Island in Washington State. I couldn't believe it was happening again.

CHAPTER 14

IT was barely daybreak when I sat on a ferry on my way to my first visit with Bill. McNeil Island loomed ahead, enshrouded in mist. It was cold, and the air struck my face, moist and chilling. I had a feeling of foreboding. I did not want to visit my husband. I did not want to sit in another prison.

McNeil was nothing like Terminal Island. It was a work farm, and there were rolling green hills with trees and the sound of the ocean always a breath away. Bill took my hand and led me to a grassy spot under a tree. He turned me by the shoulders so that I faced him. He pushed me down to my knees and knelt in front of me. "Rosalie," he said. "I love you."

I sighed in exasperation. I thought he was joking.

"I know it's hard for you to believe it. I know I haven't acted like it. Can you forgive me? Let's not hold on to old hostilities. Let's go on. Look ahead. We have our whole lives ahead. I understand now, Rosalie. I see your value. You're like an iron butterfly. You seem sometimes like you're flitting around but you're not. You've always been strong. Maybe stronger than me."

Was this the same man who barely spoke to me just a few weeks ago, on the outside, before prison? What had happened to him?

"Just be with me now, Ro. Relax. We won't think. Later, we can think. Just enjoy being here with me and I'll enjoy you. Look at this beautiful day. Remember how we used to sit on the water before we married. Victoria would be asleep in the car? Poor kid. She had no idea. Twenty-two years. We've made it a long time. God, we grew up together."

The sun was trying to break through the clouds. We stood up and strolled around. It was turning into a lovely day. My neck felt stiff. I'd been working hard. Bill was right. What harm was there in trying to relax and enjoy?

The next day was much the same. Bill did not leave my side. He held my hand, or rested his hand on my knee or an arm across my shoulder. I was suspicious. Did he need something from me? Finally, when I was about to leave, I broached the subject: "What's the matter, did something happen between you and Donna?"

I knew she hadn't left him because she was on his list for visitors and was staying in his brother's house.

"Donna's my secretary," Bill said. "We're good friends. She's been loyal to me and my family. I need her on my side."

I didn't realize at the time that in his own way and in his own veiled language he was leveling with me. Donna might be called on to testify and Bill needed her in his corner.

"We can start over," Bill said.

"I don't know if I believe that anymore," I said.

"Just pray and trust to God. Just let it be. It'll happen. We love each other. It has to. There's so much more between us besides you and me."

As I sat on the ferry back to the mainland, the sun setting fuchsia against the water, all I could think was that I don't know what to think.

Bill might have had these feelings before he went to prison. Maybe he'd discovered them when I'd gone off to Florida and he was left alone for a month, much like the time back in Arizona when I'd left with my mother and he'd severed his relationship with Erica in my absence. But my husband waited until the time was right for *him*. When he was lonely in prison. Only then did he tell me what I'd needed to hear.

Then followed poems and letters, two, three, four a week. Now I knew what I'd been missing from Bill all those years, and what the other women had probably been receiving. I understood now what they'd seen in my husband. For the first time in my life, I knew what it was like to be loved by Bill Bonanno.

Dearest Rosalie,
Seven and a half hours more and I'll be able to talk to you again. It seems today just didn't want to go by. Tonight I got two letters from you and when I got to my cubicle I was

like a kid. (It feels good to be "normal" for a change. I realize now what I have been missing all these years. I don't want it ever to change. I've heard of people being born again but I never really thought it would happen to me. Everything I do, everything I feel seems to be new and different. Especially how I feel about you.) Sometimes I lose you in the clouds. I then go about my business, searching for other people, and I become so involved that I forget that your beauty, your being, your sensual feelings nurture me to be sensitive and understanding. What you are, totally, helps me so much to be what I am now, what I will strive to be and what I am becoming.

I don't care if you write long letters or short ones; I don't care how you write or if you feel you're communicating. What I want to hear from you is that you want, understand and accept my love and devotion. That you'll give me the opportunity to love and cherish you the way I should have over the one score and two years of our life together.

Sweetheart, let it happen, drift with the waves, ride the stars and flow through space. Relax! Our love will happen if you let it. Both of us have the potential of becoming a carrier of peace and love; within the being of both of us is a gift, but it doesn't become a gift until it is given. By giving this gift we can share a feeling that will make us complete; we will

*enjoy an encounter which is as total as the
mountains, the sea, the wind, and life itself.
Please, Rosalie, realize that you possess this
inner wonder, as I do, and only by sharing
can you and I give our gifts of peace and love.
Let's not pretend. We need each other! Don't
feel inadequate. Just let it go. Think of me
each day as I think of you; each night put me
into your thoughts as I put you into mine, and,
lo, it is done. I love you and you love me—
that's it. Simple and to the point. You will
have a life of companionship, abundance and
harmony. These will be my gifts to you.*

*I have so much to make up for. So many
wrongs to right, so many pieces to put together. I want the chance, sweetheart. God
works in odd ways sometimes and I truthfully
don't know how it happened; but I just know
that suddenly I was possessed by a need, or
want, and a love for you.*

*Maybe you considered our marriage more
of a merger before this. But this will now be
a true marriage. I promise it.*

Write—
Yes, as "never" before
I love you
Bill

I'd never once thought of our marriage as a
merger. But maybe Bill had. Why else would he
have said it? Had our marriage been nothing more
than a political alliance for him, from the begin-

ning? The uniting of the once great Profacis and
Bonannos?

Perhaps. But not now. Bill, I believed, did love
me. Having Bill love me and tell me the things he
told me was all I'd ever wanted, all those years. It
filled me with sadness. It had come too late. I
searched my heart and there were no feelings but
sympathy and regret. I felt sorry for Bill and sorry
for me. But I was too fearful to allow romantic
love.

I loved Bill like family, but I did not want the
life he gave me. I wrote back to him, "I don't think
I can live up to your expectations. I love you
enough to want to see you happy. It may seem to
you now that I can make you happy, but I never
have been able to do that before, and I doubt I'm
capable of it now."

Slowly through the months and the letters Bill
began to hear me. He wrote:

> Last year I said to you, "I wonder if I love
> you enough to let you go?" I guess I finally
> found the answer. I think I wrote in one letter
> that I offered you myself, you accepted and
> returned something I could never give, or
> take, your love. I have watched you grow
> from insecurity to acceptance of life, of your-
> self. You have learned to express your emo-
> tions rather than smothering or denying them.
> You understand and have learned to com-
> municate your understanding to me and to
> others. We find meaning in life not only

*through happiness but also through sorrow.
Accept your sorrow, learn from it and grow.
It has always been easier for me to relate to
your sadness than your happiness, maybe because there has been more sadness created by
me. Whenever you came with problems, you
needed me and I became involved. But when
you shared happiness, I was left out.*

*In my own way, you will always be in my
heart and have a special place all to yourself.
But, the truth, as we both know it, is that I'm
me and you're you, oil and water, gasoline
and matches, stars and sunshine, night and
day, hot water and cold glass.*

Bill never said the words *separation* or *divorce*,
but as the letters got sadder and more resigned I
began to contemplate what life would be like without Bill. At first I thought I'd have to control myself as I'd always done while Bill was in prison. I
would not think about sex and soon I would forget
what it was like and not even want it. But in the
back of my mind there lurked a hope. Perhaps one
day there'd be another.

Still, I wrote to Bill. Bill wrote to me. We were
possessed by each other. I told him of the old feelings of resentment, of the realization of where his
priorities were (that, as he'd said so many years
ago, he was married to something else first), of my
memories of all the times we moved our family, of
the money hardships we constantly faced, and that
our whole life-style—the trials, the publicity, the

mystery of where he disappeared to, the way I never wanted to know or to face what he actually did with his days—made it impossible to go on as if nothing had happened. Bill responded. This was one of Bill's last.

> *Dear Rosalie,*
> *. . . Where do we go from here? Yes, my days are numbered in more ways than one. I guess the bittersweet truth is that our relationship has entered an inevitable, miserable terminal stage characterized by mutual despair and insurmountable obstacles. The key issue is not the extent of our problems but our willingness to work on them. I had thought it possible, with persistence and good will, to reach a place beyond resentment, a place where concord would not be banality and harmony not the simple absence of discord. The persistence and good will seems to have played out and perhaps it is time. The old feelings, which in looking back you speak of, and the "hardships" you speak of, you say remind you of my "true priorities." It's easy to cry that you're beaten, it's easy to crawl, but to fight when hope's out of sight, that's the best time of them all. It's easy to die when you come out of each grueling bout, all broken, beaten, and scarred—it's to keep on living that's hard.*
> *Life is quickly slipping away. You speak in your letters of freedom of choice, freedom to*

want no part of the past, freedom not to have it the way it was. You have been determined to be your own person—you are your own person now, I guess, and I hope that brings you happiness. You have been searching all over for happiness not realizing that he who seeks afar for happiness will not find it. It stands a guest unheeded at your very door, close behind you.

The doubts you still have are deep and maybe they can never be erased.

Tomorrow, my appeal is being heard in Washington, D.C. Maybe by the time you get this letter I'll have an answer for you. [About when I could expect his release.] I know you don't like surprises; I'll try not to give you any.

Father's Day, 1979. It's so cold, gray and windy. It's so lonesome.

Bill

The last poem he sent made me cry.

> . . . dream world
> Although tears dry
> With the passing years
> And time moves on,
> I have never been
> The same since finding you.
>
> I have searched
> For someone to replace

My dream-world of yesterday
But you never find
What you want if
You try to create it.
It must happen, without
Expectations or demands.

No one could live up
To the ideal I had
Of you, not even you.

It's very lonely.
I become close;
But then I move away,
Safe within my shell
Of broken dreams.

Bill could have been writing for both of us. And after that letter, we may not have had the papers, but we were separate emotionally and physically.

When Bill was released in May 1980, nearly two years after he was interned, he did not come home to live. He sometimes came to Sunday dinner, or called to let me know that he'd be over that night to eat, and to tell the kids to be there. But that was it.

If our children were upset by this they never let on, except for Gigi. "God, Ma," she said. "I'd rather tell people Dad was in jail than you're getting a divorce."

"We're not getting a divorce," I said.

"You might as well," she said.

She was right. And I'd resolved it in my mind.

I still went to church and still prayed to God each day, and I'd decided, as I said before, that if God forgives sins then he also must forgive mistakes. If Bill ever decided to set me free, God would forgive me.

My children had survived it all. They were doing well. Chuck had his own mechanic's shop and Joseph and Tore had been working since they came of age, Joseph at Jack-in-the-Box and Tore at Togo's. Now Joseph was in college in Tucson, and Tore was president of his class at Bellarmine.

Gigi was not a school lover, but she did well enough. Her real talent was with children. She baby-sat every night she wasn't working at the department store. And she was a friend to me.

Meanwhile, the Organized Crime Strike Force had conducted an investigation into the business dealings of my husband, his brother, and my father-in-law. It had indicted Bill's father for trying to obstruct the investigation. The trial was in progress in San Jose, and Bill was working day and night on it.

Again, the Bonanno name was all over the papers.

My immediate boss at the title company had kept me on the job because he felt a certain amount of loyalty, having seen me make my way up through the ranks for nine years. Besides, he liked me, he knew my financial situation and that I needed the job, and he respected the fact that I'd always tried to do my best. But the higher-ups were sick of the newspapers saying, "Rosalie Bonanno, who works for First American Title," especially since it was my signature that went on the preliminary title reports. Inevitably, because of all the publicity from this and the preceding trials, my boss was ordered to let me go and I lost my job.

I refused to let this setback get me down. I found a job selling the microfiche system we had used in our office. I worked on commission and made an office of my living room. In fact, I became a successful salesperson.

When Bill was let out of jail, he immediately went to work on his father's trial. He met every day with the lawyers and attended court. When he visited me and the kids, he seemed downcast and quiet, more tired than I'd ever seen him. His father was stuck in court, while his mother was very ill back in Arizona. For the first time in a long time, I tried to empathize. How many of his decisions had been made because his father had schooled him in the old tradition? What choices would he have made if he'd had his life to live as he chose? How much had he and his father spent on lawyers over the years? Joseph Bonanno and Bill could support an entire law firm with their trials. If he and his father were breaking laws and making money doing it, it was just being poured right back into the legal system. It didn't make sense, any of it.

My feelings of empathy ended when I was shocked into rage by a headline: WITNESS SAYS SHE LIED FOR LOVE OF BONANNO. Donna had been

called to testify at Mr. Bonanno's hearing. She said
that she'd begun a relationship with Bill Bonanno
shortly after he hired her in November 1976. She
said she had helped move records from Bill's business but had told the grand jury investigating the
business that she hadn't known where the records
were. "I was kind of protective," she said. "I love
him. It was a natural instinct to do it."

There it was in black and white. For all the
world to see.

I was dizzy with disgust.

Bill came over that night.

"Rosalie," he said, "I'm sorry. We made the decision with the lawyers. Krieger [the lawyer] tried
to call you, to warn you, but you weren't home. It
was for my father. He could go to jail. I had no
choice."

"You make me sick," I said. "I am so humiliated. I feel dirty. You dragged me through the gutter with you."

"Don't you think it's as humiliating to me?"

I didn't. But I said nothing. I was through.

Chapter 15

BILL's father was convicted of conspiracy to obstruct justice a few months later, and his mother died soon after that. Bill was more withdrawn and depressed than I have ever seen him.

We went to Tucson as man and wife. This was for appearance's sake. As we sat at the wake, I was overwhelmed by memories. Fay Bonanno had been nothing but kind to me. We'd shared a similar life; we'd both married Bonanno men. I wished we'd talked about it. I wished I'd been able to confide in her. But Bill was her son. I could not burden her. He'd never forgotten holidays, her name day, or her birthday. He sent her flowers every Valentine's Day. She loved him very much.

Mrs. Bonanno had been my confirmation godmother. There was a picture of us standing together on that day, a pained smile on my face, because Bill wasn't there. He was sick with mastoids.

Bill sat next to me through the wake and at the funeral and cemetery. He never cried. He was controlled as ever. As diminished as I knew he felt by this loss, as sad as he must have been, I sensed the same stature as always, the same strength emanating from him. He seemed beautiful in the way things are beautiful when they are exactly what God meant them to be.

He was gracious to the other mourners. He held up his aunt Marion. He stood next to his father. A support. The loyal son. How difficult it must be to be Bill Bonanno.

When the days were done, we went to the motel room together. We slept in the same bed. He waited for me. I waited for him. Neither of us made the first move. We did not hold each other. We hardly spoke.

It was soon after his mother's death that he gathered me and our children together to tell us he was leaving in an attempt to get his "head together," and he went to Mexico.

There was more publicity after he left. He was one of five persons indicted and accused of felony, grand theft, and conspiracy to commit grand theft. The total amount when all was said and done came to $43,000. He was the only one convicted.

I'd had it. I filed for divorce.

Given the way we'd been distant and the fact that our kids were grown—Tore had begun college and Gigi was the only child still in high school— I believed that Bill would let me do it. My filing, instead, brought the phone call from Bill in Mexico.

Then followed months of seduction, of Bill's beseeching me not to give up, of Bill's reminding me of all that we'd been through and of the commitment we'd made before God. He told me he needed my strength. But I resisted. I resisted with every ounce of will in my body. I never wanted to believe my husband again. It would only mean more hurt.

In essence, I felt held a captive in Mexico once I went down there. Bill did allow me to go home once or twice to check on the kids and the house and to sell some jewelry to cover household expenses while I was not working. When I came home I'd try to make up for lost time in my work, but it was useless. Within a few days in San Jose, I'd be getting calls again from Bill's cousin Nino telling me to go to Good Samaritan Hospital at such and such a time, and there Bill would be on the other end, commanding me back.

When he refused to let me return home at all, I tried to escape, but he'd caught me before I even boarded the bus. He complained that I never could accept him or the way things really were. He urged me to relax.

So I relaxed. I stopped harping on him every day to let me go, and he let me return to San Jose. I saw that Gigi, who was still home and living with Chuck—while Joseph had just entered medical school and Tore college—was fine, in fact very capable and happy to be left on her own.

This time when I returned from San Jose I brought a carful of kitchen appliances to make a real home with Bill in Mexico. It was clear he would never let me go, so I might as well surrender and try to make something of our life together, which did seem possible there.

Bill seemed so different. For one thing, he was bearded and tanned and relaxed. I imagine he had little or no contact with that other world, and so he had little stress. Together we meandered through afternoons. Time was generous there. The sky clear, the air warm. I relaxed into enjoying our lovemaking, which was spontaneous and wild and often. I was forty-five years old, but I looked and felt youthful and, almost miraculously, I began to experience hope.

Bill, through his constant attentions and obvious need of me, had won his way back into my heart. He seemed more vulnerable than I'd ever seen him before. Those four months of traveling in a foreign country, almost penniless and practically friendless, had humbled him. He had a new softness around his eyes, especially when he looked at me. I had almost given up on the possibility of romance in my life. And this renewal was like finding a well when you'd resigned yourself to dying of thirst in the desert.

Bill had no legal obligation to return to the United States, and because of this I had a plan. Bill could find a job in Mexico, maybe become partners with his restaurant-owner friend Saro, while I commuted to San Diego. I'd get a job and be able to stay at times with Tore. This could be the new simple life I was waiting for. We were both middle-aged now. We could grow old together in another country.

There was one hitch. Bill wanted to ask Aunt Marion to sell her house. Maybe she would give us some of the money since we'd paid the mortgage for ten years. It would be me who would have to endorse the check because of the IRS. I did not want to do this. I protested. I pleaded that I needed the security of that house. It was like our own home. I'd lived there for a long time. It held a lot of memories. I loved it. Bill could not understand my attachment. We'll get another house. A better one. You just said you'd live here with me, what do you need a place in California for?

It was important for Bill to see me give up the house. To prove to him I was committed to this new life in Mexico, with him. It was as though he wanted to destroy every little thing about my life in order to start a new one with him.

"What about Gigi, where will she live?" I protested.

"She's got a million relatives. Or, if you want, we can rent her a place. Trust me," he said. "We need the money. I know what I'm doing."

If I was going to try for a new beginning, I guessed I could do it all the way. I decided to trust my husband. Mexico would help us be different. In Mexico there would be no grand juries, no IRS, no previous convictions fouling up our chances to live a normal life.

But, sadly, Bill was kidnapped by Mexican police and released on the American side of the border, where he was arrested by the FBI.

The morning those men pinned Bill to the floor and held a gun to either side of his head was the first time in my life I'd ever seen actual physical violence done to my husband, and it haunted me for months.

When I heard him yell from the van as it rolled out of sight, "Rosalie, I love you!" I didn't run to the van and kiss him good-bye. I didn't yell, "I love you too, Bill." As my husband disappeared once again from my life, I regretted all those things I didn't do.

I remained in Mexico, waiting for some word from Bill, from his cousin Nino, from Bill's lawyers, from anyone who could tell me what to do. Tore visited for the first couple of days, and we walked on the beach. We took long drives through the hills. He did his homework and I cooked and cooked because it was Thanksgiving and I'd brought so much food down to Mexico for the holiday.

Once Tore left I spent my evenings tossing and turning and staring at the ceiling, and my days fussing around with household chores, writing my feelings in a journal and reading prayers. I washed and ironed clothes that had been stored in a suitcase. I waited and waited for someone to call. Finally, four or five days after Bill had been taken away, I heard from his lawyer that he was being held in Oakland with a one-million-dollar bail. He would have to stay in prison until he and the lawyers and whoever else was involved could get it reduced to an affordable figure.

I told myself, and did believe, that there was a perfect outcome to every situation in life because God was in charge. This trouble too would have a perfect outcome. Things would work out. I trusted in God.

I took long walks on the beach and climbed up rocks trying to exhaust my body and keep my mind calm. Then one morning, at the very beginning of December, as I stepped out of bed and glanced out the window, I saw men in white coats searching through my garbage. This was the second time since Bill had been taken away that this had happened and I lost my cool. I screamed out the window, "Get the hell away from my garbage! What I throw out of my house is none of your business. It's disgusting. You make me sick." They left and I never saw them come back.

But by that display I knew I was hoarding anger. It killed me not to know what was happening in the States. Most of the time I couldn't get hold of people, and when I did they knew nothing. I had never felt so alone. I took it as a test of autonomy, knowing that all we really have is ourselves and God.

But I was tiring of waiting. I began to pack. I said this to myself as I wrapped glasses in newspapers: "God's way is not for us to figure out. He wants us all to be home together for Christmas and for you, Bill, to be at your son Joseph's college graduation and your daughter's high school graduation. He wants you to help me sort things out and put my life in order so that when you get this thing over with there will be a good life for us together. He wanted you to get this last problem behind you so that we wouldn't have to leave our kids and live alone and isolated in Mexico. In the end it will work out."

The lawyers called and said they needed me for a bail-reduction hearing and I went crazy. "No way!" I screamed. I did not want to appear in court for any reason ever again. I began to think negatively, to get paranoid. I couldn't help myself. *Please, please don't let the money from the house go to lawyers*, I thought. *Don't use me again, Bill. I will not carry your burden. I'm falling. I'm fighting despair. I need something to hang on to. Don't hang on to me. Let me go.*

Finally, on December 4, I left Mexico.

Bill's bail eventually was reduced to $100,000, without my testimony. We needed to live in San Jose while his trial went on and until Gigi graduated. We rented the house back from the new owner.

I was very low. There was no way I could stand in front of people and sell anything. I let my job go. Eventually we started to go to Tucson to check on Bill's father's house, since he was now in prison for conspiring to obstruct justice. Bill felt good in Tucson. He wanted it to be his home, and I was loath to leave my family in California. But when I began to see the way things would go, regardless of my own preferences, I figured that if I must live in Tucson, at least it should be on my own terms. I agitated for my own home, with a mountain view and a big piece of the sky.

And that's what Bill arranged.

I live in that house in Tucson now. It's a lovely home, large enough for entertaining yet small enough to keep neat and clean. I drive a yellow

Cadillac with a telephone in it for my husband to use when he is home. He spends half of his time up in California, where he goes daily to his lawyers' offices. Nine years later, he is still working on proving himself innocent of the grand-theft charge. He was convicted but has appealed the conviction all the way to the Supreme Court, which has agreed to hear his case. My husband has written briefs. My husband has filed motions behind the scenes. If he never became a lawyer by education or profession, he's become one in practice. He travels everywhere now with a beeper on his belt and a portable telephone in his hand. Often, when he receives phone calls, he goes into the other room. If his income has soared, I wouldn't know; I am satisfied with what he gives me.

Bill says he wants to grow old with me. Bill says he has never loved anyone as he loves me and that he'll never leave me. I believe him. We have been married for thirty-three years.

My greatest joy and sense of satisfaction comes from my children. They have taken the best from me and the best from Bill. From Bill they have learned great self-confidence and a sense of loyalty and fidelity to their friends and family. From me they learned a moral soundness, candor, and integrity. My children's successes have brought me much pride and the feeling that my hard work and dedication to them has been well worth it. They call me more than once a week and visit on holidays.

At twenty-five, Gigi runs her own successful

preschool, which has been her dream since she was ten years old. I love it when she gets the students to sing my favorite song, "Sing," on my telephone machine. Tore is an executive at a very successful and innovative computer company and has just earned his MBA. Once his boss invited him and his wife, Deborah, to dinner, and Tore had to decline. It was for a Wednesday evening, and Wednesdays are reserved for dinner with his grandmother Profaci, a tradition started in previous years and continued by Tore. As Bill would say, he had his priorities straight.

Joe is finishing his medical residency in Phoenix. He is a pediatrician. He has a lovely wife, Kathleen, who gave up stockbrokering to have their sons, Salvatore and Joseph Jr. Salvatore is big and sturdy for his two years. He kisses me full on the lips every time I see him. In his deep voice, he croons, "Hug you, Gramma RoRo." Joey, at six months, delights in pulling my earrings. I call him our little Gerard because we prayed to Saint Gerard for his successful birth just as I had prayed for his father's.

Tore's daughter Jillian is bright-eyed and very vocal. She has a mind of her own but her grandfather can sway her. He makes her stop fussing with the authority in his voice. I love to see her perched in the crook of Bill's arm. She loves to walk in tall grass and ride on the back of her daddy's bike.

Chuck is the only one of my children who hasn't married. He lives in his grandfather's house. Chuck is the most creative of my children. He can visualize and build anything. He can work with metal as if it were clay. He comes by every day for dinner. He fixes everything in my house, of course, and before Bill leaves for California, he always tells Chuck, "Watch out for your mother."

But I worry about my oldest. Maybe, in his own good-humored way, he's been too busy playing guardian to me and substitute father to his brothers and sister to make a real life for himself. When Joe was applying to medical school, money was scarce, so Chuck paid for all his applications. He bought Gigi and Tore their first cars.

Together Chuck and I have bought a little plot of land in Douglas, Arizona. I think it makes us feel more secure, even though when we took a drive to see it one day we couldn't find it. The area was overgrown with desert weeds and there were no roads. We laughed when we discovered this, then Chuck put another tape in his Jeep and the sand flew from the wheels behind us as we sped on our way back home.

I've come to love Tucson. I have good friends here, married and single. When Bill is away, I have complete freedom and privacy. For a while I was a real estate agent, then looked for a job in my property-related computer field but now I'm starting my own business making bridal veils.

There's a view of a mountain from my house. It changes color every minute. I love to sit in my backyard and watch it as the clouds roll past toward the horizon. I must glance at that mountain a hun-

dred times a day wherever I am in the city. It makes
me feel that no matter how confused and unsteady
and changeable my life has been, it was all on the
surface, due to conditions changing around me, but
deep inside, underneath, I've been like that mountain, unchanging. Simple. Even strong. I love my
family. I have my memories, and I have the life
that's ahead. In the end, I don't know if I've accepted so much as learned to live with the con-
straints of my life. I like to think that, through it
all, I've been there for Bill and my children, and
that's what's important.

Bill and I were born into an ancient tradition that
was carried to America from Sicily. This tradition
has meant different things and some of the same
things to both of us. For me it meant a large, warm
family, where I was protected by a strong father
and lived so cloistered that I could venture into the
world only if escorted by a male of my own blood.
I was educated by pious nuns who contributed to
my feelings of being protected and secure. I was
sure of my role as a woman, which meant, eventually, to be a wife and mother. I was not prepared
to deal with the outside world as it really was. I
never even questioned the fact that my father cen-
sored the newspaper before his children were per-
mitted to read it. This was *my* tradition, a cocoon
of warmth, security, protection, and continuity that
stretched back almost a thousand years to medieval
Sicily.

Bill was raised to be a warrior prince in a secret

society. For him the philosophy of life and the life-style he believes in and lives by stand for honor, integrity, and loyalty. He has sworn his allegiance to his father and his fidelity to a larger family. I could see this sometimes, and other times I chose to insulate myself from my husband's world.

He once told me an old Sicilian legend. It's said that the word *mafia* originated when the invading soldiers carried off a young Sicilian girl to rape her. Her mother ran through the streets crying, "*Ma fia, ma fia*" ("My daughter, my daughter"). The Sicilian men in the village went to the girl's rescue and the name *mafia* was born. My husband says it was a secret organization that righted wrongs.

Bill does not see himself as a lawbreaker but as a legal keeper of an older form of justice. That this meant a life of crime in the eyes of U.S. law-enforcement agencies and the U.S. courts was, for Bill, simply the way it had to be. His greatest wrath is reserved for those Sicilians who turn their backs on the tradition like soldiers deserting a field of battle.

I could never accept the lawlessness, violence, danger, and death the tradition carries with it. I think in his way Bill would have liked to share more with me, but I wouldn't allow it. Bill knew I did not want to be involved in this part of his life and he did not insist that I do so. I am grateful to him for that, but my blindness has cost me a lot.

I wanted to be ordinary and to have people ac-cept me for me. There may be hundreds of Sicilian wives who are caught up in the old traditions, and then there may be many who have broken away. Surely there are others like me who have straddled both ways. I tried to be a computer programmer, a real estate agent, a title officer, a den mother, and a Sicilian wife.

I could never accept or approve of my husband's world. I have suffered because of my nonacceptance; I have also grown because of it.

At first Bill was disappointed in me because I never maintained an interest in the other side of his life, but later he allowed me to be involved by letting me do my own thing, and I appreciated that. I always submit to my husband's strength. He has given me security, and I have given him his freedom to live his life-style.

I live day to day waiting for my cowboy to resume his life in Tucson. I love God. I have faith in His scheme of things. I have learned that in life, we never reach utopia but are always on the way, venturing, risking. I have resolved to make the best of my situation and be happy. Bill is right. To expect what I consider a normal life is to live in a fantasy world.

I am tied to my husband. By tradition, yes. By our vows, certainly. But mostly by a love that won't go away.